uDam Skippy

uDam Skippy

A gentleman smuggler Offloads Vibes & Victory

SKIPPY RAST

PALMETTO
PUBLISHING
Charleston, SC
www.PalmettoPublishing.com

Copyright © 2024 by Skippy Rast

All rights reserved

No portion of this book may be reproduced, stored in a retrieval system, or transmitted in any form by any means—electronic, mechanical, photocopy, recording, or other—except for brief quotations in printed reviews, without prior permission of the author.

Paperback ISBN: 979-8-8229-4153-3

Contents

Introduction: And Away We Go 7
Chapter 1: Calling All Cars in the Vicinity 13
Chapter 2: Hot Fun in the Summertime 18
Chapter 3: First Toke over the Line 20
Chapter 4: We Got to Move Those Microwave Ovens 25
Chapter 5: Entertaining through the Painful Truth 29
Chapter 6: Reach for the Preach 31
Chapter 7: PAGING: All Square Ds 38
Chapter 8: You Gotta Fight for Your Right 41
Chapter 9: How Appropriate, That Number Nine, #9, #9, #9 45
Chapter 10: The Granny Effect 48
Chapter 11: Let's Rat Lawyers in Love 51
Chapter 12: First Cane Pearly Gate, Big Fish 55
Chapter 13: Simply L 76
Chapter 14: More Fun, More Funding 79
Chapter 15: Not in My DNA 85
Chapter 16: The Four Knots to Blossom 94

Chapter 17: Numbers, Baby: 12K Flight 105

Chapter 18: Get Outta Jail Free...113

Chapter 19: Be Scene, Not Herd: In Lieu of Bud Rose.....................122

Chapter 20: Paging Earnie 126

Chapter 21: In the Meantime..132

Chapter 22: Mandy for the Moment...146

Chapter 23: Show Me the Money 159

Chapter 24: Soft Intro to JJ 166

Chapter 25: More Antics from the Joanster..171

Chapter 26: Why They Call Agents Special?......................................184

Chapter 27: Jury Trials, Military Brash, and Hawkins.....................188

Chapter 28: Heroes and Fed Readies 193

Chapter 29: Can't Seize This 201

Chapter 30: Last First Date 207

Chapter 31: A Solitary Man..211

Chapter 32: What Are Your Lottery Odds Anyway? 220

Chapter 33: Choppin' It Up on the Lam...224

Chapter 34: Can I Whine Just a Little?...233

Chapter 35: All Good Things Must Pass: Bye-Bye............................236

Introduction
And Away We Go

There's no use in painting the window, 'cause nobody wants to look in
Some face might some fake ass, some bimbo, no gentleman loser again.

So, you maybe thinking about looking into it? Well, they call me Skippy, and welcome to my write. "uDam Skippy," they cried (aka the Gentleman Smuggler). Well, not *the* gentleman smuggler but rather just one of the many referred to as gentlemen smugglers (GS). This alias was granted to the group of us partly by the press and by the Feds in hopes of sparking more interest in such irresponsible responsible types for smuggling a mountain of weed back during the eighties. That we might assume more relevance suitable for the detailed pursuit soon to follow. Personally, I considered both the "gentleman" and the "smuggling" tags a bit embellished and might add that the "gentleman" part came about much more easily than did the "smuggler" one. As one of the true smugglers once lamented subsequent to our being dubbed the gentlemen smugglers at the time, "[That label] is certainly preferred over some other less complimentary nameplates. I mean, they could have called us 'asshole smugglers.' So yeah, we'll go with the 'gentleman' one every day."

My foray into this underworld magic carpet ride wasn't anywhere near "major dude" level or the kingpin level; mine was more a journey of sorta falling into some kinda sky, y'all. So this write would be from the perspective of being totally out of the loop but somehow finding oneself in it, in the thick of it, nonetheless. I'd hope and even pray for a shot at the easy money, for a shot to step up to the plate just to see if there might be any contact. Not all that careful with what I wished for, either. Lemme attempt to make some sense of it, OK? And since it's from the personal standpoint of observation and education rather than said conclusions emanating from or representing in any manner the group of us, the grit rippers of us, the more appropriate title is *uDam Skippy*. Not an alter ego. Not tryin' to get dropped off either. I wish to arrive. That's all. Don't wish to go back. Just a guy with a peculiar mindset, which I'm delighted to discover. One that required much reshuffling and falling back a bit, relying upon gut, grit, and gratitude. One whereby the meshing of resistance and acceptance could dwell and celebrate together in peace. Hey people, expending our precious energy in areas of irrelevance simply drains us and serves up zero benefit. We live a grand life, and once we identify as much—the larger picture, if you will—surely it will enable a more balanced approach toward the mindset of contentment. Release the hounds.

And first up? Are you offended by foul language? Go do something else. For some of us less formally educated gentleman lacking the broader vocabulary, submitted herein for your discovery, we shall indeed uncover an abundance of "shits," "asses," and even a few "dicks" slung about as we proceed. Further, as for the ole f-word...I choose to launch it on occasion as well. So fcuk it. Fock it. Or FM, FU, or fokQ. This you may denounce amid my many whims (or translate it if you must as "feel me?" and "frontin' up" what they do). However, kindly process the following statement with emphasis: every profane reference presented to you simply depicts circumstances under which events actually occurred or the mindset in which they happened and were processed at the time. And usually such events occurred during rather tense observations, mostly overly exaggerated takes and depictions to begin with. The pomp and circumstance offered up—if you will, again—is only meant in the nicest possible manner. So when you spot yet another FU somewhere, another fokQ someplace else...take solace, OK, because after all, "Hey, he means all that nonsense in the nicest possible manner, right?"

See there? Clouds in my coffee, baby. Now you're getting it. Besides, such descriptions, commonly referred to as "woofin'" or "boostin' up" in the first place, are common ego and prison lingo live-bys suggesting the perpetrator is attempting to project. That toughness and mystique when in real time there's a bunch more bark than bite, both of which are rendered mostly harmless and more the genuine chickenshit sling-bys to begin with. Just so we flocking get it. All the tough guys come from much harder time than they currently occupy.

Speaking of real time and of the real rick, here's a mild example. Let's suppose you're the one aboard a shrimp trawler stuffed with 20K pounds of weed. What the hell are you doing there? How did you get there? Yeah.

Me too. Suddenly, *bam*, a set of coast guard stripes appear on the horizon. Now what? Anybody? Somebody? Everybody? "Aw, shucks!" wasn't exactly the terminology being bantered about there. Not part of any throw down of that particular instant. Can I get an "oh shit!" please? As it really was, please? "Yikes, stripes." As it really freaking was? Now there is a true "Feel me."

Within the scope of these recollections we realized the vivid imaginations or knack for a certain creativity people might actually wish to review rendered not quite as necessary

Now, all this said, should you foster a certain uneasiness over mere words, please seek comfort elsewhere, with those more so inclined to conformity cluttered amid the many universal boundaries so implied or imposed. Might we peel back just a touch of the cult of never-ending personalities and strive as one—or at least attempt—to embrace an outcome? Which may include more of us? Ask yourself, like I finally did, What does it matter to me what another thinks? I'm still able to sleep and carry on the next day for as long as those days may seek the next sunrise. Meaning, all people are allowed their own thoughts, correct? If your world is one of rainbows, unicorns, and puppies, just stop it already. Back to Shut-Your-Facebook go you, maintaining proper mental distance from those like me. After all, freedom of association is an absolute right of yours too. "uDam Skippy," he cries. While I do care about your feelings, it's just not all that much. But enough so to prepare you for the fact that the context before you is not intended for children, nor is this content offered up as to antagonize. In some circles the antics and descriptions herein might be considered so appalling as to rattle many of today's endless parade of drive-by intellectuals. Should you fall into this category where acceptance and comfort through actual deception are masked behind the semantics of betrayal, please keep on driving. Though it is unbecoming to a gentleman smuggler of sorts to confirm stereotypical assumptions, I tend to use bad language to begin with. So let's blame it on Elladnella. Or Rio. I simply want to serve you up a little "street." Some true "street" side. Therefore, mine is a different style, uncouth and disregarding of PC, the #poundmetoo type movements, the wokes, the wakes, whatever the hell—there's much deviation from these "norms," whose ever they may be. Damn sure ain't mine, and hey, guess what? Since my mommy passed, and would not approve of said vulgarity or callous insensitivities? These new age values, having assumed the more prominent position amid us the people? I'm granted cover through an ownership unimpeded. To review, assess, comment and rant minus the reins of her oversight. In real legal circles, I do believe the term being sought out here is indeed affectionately better identified as "plausible deniability." Hey, since you dealin' me in at the table, time to dole it back out. Hit me, jack.

Coming out the gate this way regarding language and misplaced terminologies may seem a bit unusual. Well, it does to me too. With emphasis, lemme say that I wasn't raised this way. To end up or be this way. To be labeled the "local hoodlum element." A criminal. Too much time on my hands. Or anything pertaining to a smuggler. A disregarding soul toward civility, gentlemanly, or otherwise. Wasn't built for crime. Wasn't built to hit that petal on the right either whenever blue lights would appear in the rearview. I chose it. I own it. And once exposed to the culture of crime and time and the nuances thereof, I suppose the culture and the dumb luck simply sucked me in. I did defy authority, mostly for the sake of defiance. Nothing personal to them or to you, you see. Nothing even so much as planned either. Simply an eagerness, a yearning to fight something. But what? Life was too easy. Too boring. Too expected. Just another runaway, mundane train. G'damn it, man. Lemme breathe, man. Lemme me gear it down and feel the RPMs kick in, and let's fcuking get there. Lemme stand next to that fence at Del Mar horse track and breathe deep into the ten tons of muscle screaming by. Just once. Don't ask why they all do it, the hundreds of jobs and people involved. Just live it, baby. Gimme those three steps. Hey, I know what. I'll fight authority. Authority sometimes wins (as the song doesn't go). However, authority has zero interest in small-town clowns the likes of my silly ass.

Chapter 1
Calling All Cars in the Vicinity

We sometimes hear many druggie types bemoan law enforcement officers (LEOs). You know that authority makes things more difficult. How do LEOs take their jobs too seriously? How do they target us and cause us angst? Well, allow me to proclaim the obvious here, just so you may slide up on some real shit. Without LEOs, there's, well... it wouldn't be a country to begin with, but aside from that, that precious weed you're trying to sling, smoke, or whatever would have very little value. Intrigue, you say? Gone. That's right. Zero hype. Zero tough guy. There is not much value if there is no risk. There is no rebellious culture either; no "bad boys, bad boys, whatcha gonna do?" The entire spectrum of weed culture loses all mystique and intrigue the instant LEOs are withdrawn from the picture, whereby pursuits are no longer any concern or threat. We're all mere drunks with no story instead. Simple enough.

That said, here's my estimation of what authority seeks out:

a) The ability to go home after their shift—hear that one and hear it again;
b) A means to make a living with as little risk as possible;
c) Fulfilling obligation to their sworn duty;
d) A degree of significance so as to compensate taxpayers for our guaranteed salaries, benefits, and retirement perks;
e) While remaining very much on point of surroundings and of opportunity as may appear for position and for some clout, for a little stroke.

They're not into the throwback programs involving the likes of me. Or you. I'm the one daring them to chase me. Deviling them to catch me (see b and e above). So don't bother painting that window either; believing "mercy" necessarily your option to determine.

During the ordeal of serving time, in most prisons the doors to cells are as depicted as the one on the cover of this book. Prison officials generally allow us leeway to a mild degree of privacy by taping a strip of cardboard just parallel to that narrow window. It's called a flap. We can close the flap for bathroom privacy or for when we wish not to be pestered by other inmates so long as prison guards may perform their frequent checks and counting of us as alive. Thus when the flap is closed, it is commonly referred to as "painting the window."

A little digress there.

Gradually, one comes to realize after living on that criminal edge for a while, then cribbin' up there on a full-time basis, that the new mindset begins to get good to ya, which, as a natural evolution, gets better for ya once one stokes it a little more and more. Down the rabbit hole, you go a-tumbling. All jacked-back and tricked-out. Then one day you peep your head out above ground, and it hits you. Attributable, at least in this case, to the independence of it all. Although based upon the complete fantasy it is, what's notable here is that, hey, suddenly there's no having to answer to anyone. And, hey, can't be fired either. Whoa. Can maybe be stopped. But can't be fired. So you see, this criminal lifestyle did seem to offer up a little more than I might have assumed going in. It granted me complete freedom, which I had never experienced prior for lack of grit, of confidence, and of funding. For most like me, this revelation itself is an unexpected byproduct of the risk, affording a more gradual acceptance of said risks, daring me and likely many others to take bigger bites of that forbidden fruit.

Independence is a powerful tool. There are many other means by which to achieve complete freedom. But lemme tell you one thing, OK? Take that longer way around, would you please? The criminal way compels one to ignore the fueling of the runaway freight train rumbling blindly down the mountainside, as with yours truly, the clueless conductor shoveling more and more coal just to see how far we can push it really good. Going off the rails on a crazy train. People are lining the tracks, wishing it were them the one minute, then utterly relieved and grateful during the next for witnessing the pile of that twisted heavy metal pipe dream strewn about there down Red Herring Lane.

Nonetheless, people suddenly realize that all "nice and nicer" was no longer required reading. All of a sudden, the need to tow their line, "the man's" line, became a routine I checked at the door. It felt great. Up until then it was somebody else's line me and many others tended to accept in exchange for bought-and-paid-for thoughts, actions, and money, or that status and approval thing. Usually aided by looking the other way as if sounds of silence couldn't be seen. Anything to deflect more noteworthy threats at hand, suggesting that all this funky shit going down in our city was "no cause for alarm;" therefore relax, everybody. Everything's cool here. Assuming the masses consider that a pleasant demeanor and structured, disciplined means of expression somehow protect the civility we relish when in reality becoming informed in terms of the real rick would certainly tend to render us stronger. Strange. Tooling along with the herd, looking the other way, and expecting rewards for complacency are rendered quite easily. Expected, even. We're unwittingly beaten into submission, completely voiding the threats requiring everyday slugs to defend that which allows civility to thrive in the first place. Before the weeds of wonderment were sewn, I'd kinda stared at the ground. Like an everyday chickenshit pecking at the dirt simply to look occupied. But then came the crime. The criminal behavior. It came easy despite this type of behavior is not expected from us. From me. And with it?

Sheer discovery. Freedom of thought. Freedom of speech. Freedom of association. There's nothing to get hung up about. Not for me. Sorry. Hey, my new job isn't based upon others perceiving my thoughts as normal or acceptable. Even today, though, I don't have to be mindful of just any image so projected, though I still throttle it way back, nonetheless.

I can still achieve setting the example rather than being made the example of.

It starts with language. Including—careful—the language used to attempt to boost up that particular image to either extreme. I heard a real rock star say one fine day that an ounce of image equals a pound of performance. And still, one must remain mindful that one slip, one misinterpreted joke or thought, and off we go, twisting in the breeze. Not so in criminal circles. For most of us most of the time, after defying such taskmasters, there comes one of those dialed up apologies. However, in the nonreal world of crime, one learns to value one of its by products more, like I said. That independence thing. And sometimes its power is so sweet that we become careless. Too damn dumb to discern good fortune amid the rarity of these times, yet allowing all these possibilities. Why choose this easy road? Oh, if only I had embraced this blessing at hand and respected its value. If only I had striven for goodness and established wisdom through hard work instead of hard knocks. If only. The story probably wouldn't possess quite as much drama, but the sense of achievement damn sure wouldn't suggest quite the degree of this-is-what-it-is slough-off either.

Chapter 2
Hot Fun in the Summertime

Oh, it's summertime on Edisto Beach. Let's suppose you're a younger person working a job at a beachside paradise in a quaint little postcard town on the coast. Sort of a dream job at the true Edisto Beach landmark. The Pavilion. You see, this Pavilion was where the action flourished and where everybody was to be found. A game room. A dance hall. Ice cream. Vacationers all drop their kids off so parents can take a break so as to enjoy their vacation too. Right? Sitting on those steps out front of the Pavilion in the early evening was pretty much our version of Facebook back then. The entire beach could know in an instant who was out and about, who the bands might be, and all that. There was even a pier on site. People were going fishing and just going out on the pier to take in the view. However, a walk down this iconic pier would cost you fifty cents. Fifty cents! Once upon a time, when my ass started working at this particular venue, on a break one day, I decided to walk down that pier and say hello to everyone. Hell, I work here now. So it's free to me, right?

Wrong. During my first free walk down my free pier on my first break working the place, who comes tooling up on his little golf cart but my ole crabby-ass boss. "Hey, Skippy. That'll be fifty cents, please."

"But I work here now; I still have to pay the fifty cents?"

"You guessed it. Still cost me for upkeep and maintenance, don't you know. Or if you don't wish to pay the fifty cents, just don't walk on my pier. Simple enough." He got his reluctant fifty cents that day and then, and there came an abrupt end to anymore long walks upon his precious short little bullshit pier.

Well, that first day didn't end up so good either. Got some nerve charging me fifty cents; I lapsed into the employee mode that everyone seemed to go through: "He doesn't appreciate me," "I'm here all the time when he's not," "I go to a lot of trouble to get here." "My boss has no idea in the hot sun thumbing my way to work." Already throws out these vibes of nonappreciation. All these cars, not a care in the world, just breezing by me like I'm some nobody. Ride, ride, ride, hitching a ride. And the wind cries Mary, people; however, I guess ole Mary doesn't lie either as another happy-go-lucky tourist breezes by me, the young broke ass they correctly perceive me to be, holding a thumb out in the air.

Oh shit, what's this coming?

Chapter 3
First Toke over the Line

A top three topic of mine. The fairer sex. And first up? A rather significant one. A very significant one. It's that little cutie-pie college girl sporting around her daddy's '63 Cadillac Coupe DeVille convertible, wrapped up, all tricked out in that beach-wide infamous purple velvet coating. No deadhead stickers on this Cadillac. Talk about no shot. Zip shot. Not even time of day in a clock shop. "Hey Nineteen" in real-life living color.

Check out this slick move that I picked up from a few years back, where I turn and face the traffic, but don't put the thumb out as if to say this is a checkout, not begging for a ride, simply more interested in the scenery and sizing you up first as thumb-worthy. There is an understatement just in time. It appears the purple velvet Cadillac is responding to the right foot on the left petal. Somebody pinch my goofy little young boy ass.

Rebecca of Sunnybrook charms whips that blond hair around and looks back, tilting the Ray-Bans on top of her head, and hollers, "Come on, Skippy, I ain't got all day!"

And no, I did not ask, "Who, me?" I eased on up and sat my ass in the shotgun rider, and off we went breezin.' Little did I know where that ride before me would lead. Diddy don't drive in that Eldorado no more.

OMG. Thank you, Jesus. Could this be the reason there's an Edisto Beach to begin with? What movie scene did this come out of? Who can handle this truth? That would be my ass. There are no awkward events in Edistopia, don't you know?

Just about then the star of the show proclaims, "Hey, Skippy, as soon as we get past Daddy's house, just might have a little surprise or two just for you."

Wow. A little surprise? Just for me? While waiting for whatever this magical star may hold, we look up, and there are a few pelicans gliding with us up the beach. It's a popular thing to do, you know, to glide up the beach, shadowing these magnifico shit machines. And as exhilarating as it's gotta be—you know, to fly, to breeze the beach fifty feet up in total silence—there's no way those creatures could be having more fun than me during this one snapshot still frozen in my data base of grayish matter; as an all-star Polaroid, it still remains.

About then her daddy's house jogs on by us. "You do smoke a little smoke, right?" Well, of course. What, you think me some sort of country dork nobody, or what? Smoke what? She's passing to me what I later discover to be what's commonly known as a roach. OK, the objective here is not to be perceived as a total klutz; are you still with me? Somehow we managed to wrestle the roach up to my lips, and therein I proceeded to take my first toke, shattering the glass of that ceiling directly above me ever so cautiously. Did you get that?

This is my first toke, my first bite of the succulent forbidden fruit. And what goes better with weed? Well, my fellow little seed poppers…that would be a strong dose of Led Zeppelin II, of course. Cranked up. And rambling on down the beach, we glide, shadowing that string of pelicans in a trick unit, with a real-life gorgeous college girl flippin' me a first trick buzz, then politely taking a very ladylike "Hey Nineteen" bow. Wow. My first experience with sex, drugs, and rock 'n' roll? Hardly. How 'bout two outta three, maybe? OK. We go with that as well.

It's second nature to remember that exact spot to this day and remember the good times. Bad times—'course I've had my share. And every single time I cruise by it, even to this day, there's that flashback. To the blaze of that balmy summer. The succulent aroma of the abundantly applied Coppertone suntan lotion identifies us all as hip. As the true beach people. We all were skinny. Healthy. No tats, no cell phones. What happened? Time happened. That simple. And oh, man-o-Manischewitz, let's not forget the BigApe. W-A-P-E Radio. The mighty 690. Our default powerhouse beaming 50,000 watts outta Jacksonville, Florida. That's right. Jacksonville, Florida. *Bitch* ass! We could get it. We did get it. As it was only 160 miles due south as the crow flies. And our beach stared in that direction, unobstructed. Nowhere else in South Carolina was there the BigApe. We were cool. United as one. Under one rock. The grandest music of a generation; several actually. Our music of the day. Also embracing the discovery of growing up and feeling like a million, lookin' like a couple more. Our culture, destiny, and the engraved invitation to limitless contentment in life. Little did we know at the time that the seed for uniqueness had indeed already been sown in us through our unique virtue. The secret to thriving within all the opportunities was discovering the entire gauntlet being revealed to us right now. Right this minute. How can it possibly get any better? Are we equipped to deal with it? How might we even process this blessing? Can we even recognize that we are part of the most blessed people ever to exist? Hey, it was a lot to digest and still is.

Ride, captain, ride upon this mystery ship; why don't ya? Anticipation. Lady Madonna. Hot fun in the summertime. Getting closer to my home. And war. What is it good for? Never been to Spain either. But we've all been to Chicago, baby. Every night. *W-L-S*. AM radio. Another rare station on the AM dial that didn't turn down the 50,000-watt transmitter after sundown. Our backdrop of nightlife. Somebody pinch me. Does anybody really know what time it is?

So you see what's happening, right? All the associations and affiliations I'm processing due to the little hottie sporting some of her daddy's stolen weed. All the while, mind you, there is the flip side. Remembering all the clatter-box from those many endearing souls truly concerned about my long-term well-being posting up as my firewall explicit instructions to stay the hell away from the dreaded contraband. What? And not get lost in your rock 'n' roll? That message, shall we say, rather lost much of its punch in these Edisto Beach days. This moment is still considered one of the grandest of this lifetime. And there have been a few. Full speed ahead. The torpedoes be damned again.

Chapter 4
We Got to Move Those Microwave Ovens

All good things must pass, as you know. Then came the dreaded back-to-work days to follow. Sometime afterward. Hey, Skippy, was that you I saw breezing down the beach with that terminally pretty one, none other than Ms. Rebecca herself? Could have been; who really knows? Turns out there's a new wag to the walk. Hey, I've been there and done that. Hey, man, 150 pounds of goofy-ass me just transitioned into a brand-new 420 pounds of swag. A steamin' hunk of heavy junk. My ass didn't just show up to work that day; didn't just fly in that day. Oh hell no. This boy arrived, yo (more on this later). This boy took wing, MFs. Suddenly life becomes the discovery of discovery itself.

Which sometime thereafter delivers me to another one of those fifteen-minute breaks on the ole job. On another break, instead of the fifty-cent throw down, I opt for a stroll up the beach to the north side, directly in front of the state park. No fifty-cent fee for that. So much for this would-be episode of pier pressure. The surf was easy on the day I came to stay strolling up the beach, just sorta in dream mode, wondering what the future may hold. Hold up a sec, everybody.

Now what in the world might this boxy-looking thing barely bobbing about in the shallows as the tide continues to ebb? Let's investigate further, shall we? About the size of a microwave oven, I guess. But wait...there's another one over there. Both were packaged in what initially I thought to be cardboard boxes but turned out to be burlap and were just sitting there on the beach. Now I've never been anywhere or done anything, but any dumb ass can tell ya what these are. Even me.

Two bales of weed. Jackpot. Say what? Yeah. It's two bales of weed. The ole square grouper. I started to shake, thinking it might be a setup. Is this some sort of test? Turns out no. It's only a couple bales of weed. How did it get there? Why did it get there? I found out and in fact created some square groupers later in my so-called career.

But wait a minute, people. It's also that fork in the road. What do we do now? Instantly I start to grind the pros and the cons. Is that ten grand sitting there? Hold on a sec. That's five years in prison sitting there also? This is easy. There're always choices, remember? Do nothing? Haven't I gathered that one Ms. Lovely Rebecca has a certain affinity for the dreaded contraband?

Shove me into shallow water here, people, before I get too deep, or go back and tell my boss and call the cops? Not. Or grab that shit and let it happen. There you have it. In the instant. Quickly, children, what do we do? Well, I guess we know the answer to that one. My protective angels allowed an open door to a velvet Cadillac, and I gladly accepted the company, the scenery, and the allure as the acceptance itself. Rip the rearview mirror off, boys, for there is no looking back at this point. Set the bridges all afire. This magic moment, this breakaway-getaway gateway, we-have-liftoff ranks as one of the most regrettable nonregrettable regrets of all time. As if I'm one in a stack of clay pigeons locked and loaded. Then suddenly, "Oh shit." Somebody just yelled, "Pull!" And oh my double shit! It's that freaking Higgins and he just don't miss.

I promptly dragged the two bales into some nearby shrubbery, went back to work, afterward driving through the state park to my stash and placing those two meal tickets in the trunk of my grandmother's borrowed Ford Falcon, and drove home after my shift. Not a care to be found. I wondered why someone would go to the trouble to smuggle weed into the country only to toss it overboard. What gives? Well, as I discovered later, most bales were washed up on sum beaches as part of a decoy, purposely sacrificed in a particular area well away from where a major haul off loading was taking place while Feds flocked to the several reports, well away from the epicenter. It worked every time, or at least we thought it did.

Well, somebody woke up that next morning a felon. A champagne supernova streaks the sky. Staring at the pine tongue-and-groove slats from my bed, the question persisted. Are people felons even once the act has been committed, though they have not been brought to task for it? Yet? Is it criminal to weigh criminal inclinations? Dear Grandmama hollering upstairs, asking if I wanted anything from the store. Oh shit. There's a couple wet bales in her trunk. "Hey, Granny, I'll be glad to go to Mellechamps for ya; give me a list." Wish there had been a couple more items on that list.

Our grandmothers, for the most part, go beyond their obligation to simply raise us and nurture us, they need to support us. And in return expect us to demonstrate that we respect their devotion and discipline, and as such the unwritten rule is that we shall honor their efforts through a humble and grateful existence. Despite a lot of silly antics perpetrated by certain of us during that age of the innocent tree-branch dwellers, grandmothers forgive and are programmed primarily through hope to support us. Hope. They hope we can make a difference. They hope we apply the character they bestow upon us as a matter of our daily routine. They know it's unlikely for them as individuals that any noticeable degree of significance in society is forthcoming. Therefore, they rely on us, through their face of loyalty, devotion, and love, to conduct ourselves in such a manner as to render our mothers proud. To cling precariously to any thought that our foundation for good due to our advantage in life through them has purpose. A dignified purpose. I failed my two mothers in this arena as they steadfastly pretended otherwise, as they could only, that I was an undercover agent drug smuggler. Had to be, right? Skippy wouldn't break the law. We raised him through virtue. My regret for ya. For failing my mothers in the extreme.

Chapter 5
Entertaining through the Painful Truth

The strategy herein attempts to inform through exploitation our insatiable fix for entertainment. Entertainment allows us to withdraw from the thinking process. And withdraw we do. The unknown or unexpected detriment to us in the quest of entertainment serves as a superb tool for some to hustle us up, basking in our void of information substituted by the seemingly permanent distraction of entertainment itself. Betcha by golly wow, if there was not in your mind at least the expectation of the slightest harvest of entertainment likely through the reading of these pages, you never would have given it a second's breath of consideration. Could be you don't rely on some slug as such for information. Hey, you gather sources for your own info, right? The bait and switch thing; you're no sap. No entertainment? What? Well, then you have better things to do. Likely coming away from the time so devoted to the expectation of fun where there is none, a bit frustrated.

I would like for my people to get it. There are some things to learn that everyday peeps might very well benefit from. To this end, should we toss in a few tales of weed in the mix, of its alleged intrigue to the mix, of piles of assumed shock and dismay to the mix? Why, all of a sudden, there is a forum. And there's some of your attention up for grabs, provided the swap for time invested reaps a degree of mild entertainment. Right? Just searching for clues at the scene of the crime, but check it now: life's been good to me so far.

Although I chewed off considerable prison time, my outlook on life isn't one of doom and gloom, nor one of spite or of how wrongly poor, pitiful little ole doofus-ass woof-ass me was treated. It did open these eyes. I am a big boy and wouldn't present tritely those times as some low-budget effort to bitch and moan, as if this world craves more of any of that useless horseshit. From anyone. Therefore, celebrate with me on the other side the notion that we all have hit the lottery of life. Absolutely the case. To be born in these times. The notion that to exist as Christian and American is the ultimate blessing on Earth, having provided us all incredible opportunities for learning, innovation, and achievement. And comfort. Through the measured concepts of our passioned yet peculiar intellect, we continue to reap the bountiful harvest of wealth and wisdom. As we continuingly discover others of this world do indeed resent the shit out of certain disciplines and abilities. Now there's some true entertainment.

Chapter 6
Reach for the Preach

What's prison really like? I'm asked this all the time. What's my take on the legal system? Did you save any money from the drug smuggling days? Was it worth it? Have any regrets?

Look, people, I get it. I committed a crime and then did some time. OK? No mystery here. Not trying to sidestep that fact. Or make light of it. Just so you know. But also know that in exchange for the crime, a considerable education was obtained. Plus, there was that able-to-retire-young deal too. At twenty-four. It was wonderful. Life was sterling. No worries, no work, no bills. Could wake up every day and decide what to go buy. Gangsta leaning down Big Boy Boulevard. I'm gonna rap on your door and tap on your windowpane. It may be a wide highway, though its length not nearly as long as the runnin' and funnin' down Big Boy Boulevard. Healthy, young, and rich. For the following twenty years. This is how we all should retire. When we're young and able to travel and experience life, during our physical prime. Then, as we slow down due to the aging process and the depletion of energy, we go to work in our forties, fifties, and sixties. Able to better focus. Able to better value time itself, not distracted by those dreadful doses—sometimes overdoses—of youthful indiscretion.

And to whatever degree you may detect or reject the "attitude," why not simply allow this to only confirm you exist in a more accepted manner, denouncing lawlessness, shock, and vulgarity. As for the exaggerated frivolities of my world, well, they are no more embellished in real time than the emptiness occupying time in yours, spinning aimlessly amid Facebook, sports radio, or the never-ending "breaking news" cycles of fires, weather, or youngsters gone wild. A bunch of bullshit that doesn't matter one single breath. For once let's label it all for what it is and call out those wound up in pursuit of opportunity afforded by the low-information morons like me and you at one time or another. Whereby the snitch, flip, characterless, culture-misguided, and celebrated slugs may not be forgiven simply through the impunity or deflection of self. From somewhere amid all the entertainment, somebody else's cash, somebody else's favorite songs, and BS fueling our worlds, please allow the process of evaluating those extremes herein to fall back a bit so as to analyze more so what actually does matter. To you. That's right. What do you allow in your house? In your world? That really matters? As significant to you. Discover your own self.

Control your own brain, man. That's right. That's spot on. You are in control as to what you allow in your space. Your head. And remember, a constant supply of repetitive information has the power to wash that brain. Even if, even if it's nontruths. The power to scrub your brain thoroughly, and sometimes while not even requiring your permission. Scary. To go so far as to wash your brain kitchen clean of logic. Often without your knowledge. Often in defiance of your own selected character too. Of intellect. Be careful, people. Define your truth as real to you prior to your granting which ever truths you so choose to occupy your mind.

You know, I was lucky to a degree in a skewed sorta trance once introduced to an undeniable truth. The penitentiary. The numbers of time itself. My realization to an absolute truth. Prison. I did indeed allow this truth to enter my brain. Hey, it was impossible not to, lemme tell ya. But seriously, that absolute truth began the pathway for me when it came to such deciding what might be allowed in. The bar for truth and what to allow in, was raised towards those truths more absolute than before. Whereby some of the prior ones based mostly on feelings or falsehoods or hope began my gradual eviction process of them. A blessing. The resulting process simply employing this higher standard of acceptance as to what might occupy my grey matter space up there. Treat this access up top as you would invoke such a standard down below. Careful what you open doors to within the sacred space of of you.

Get to something worth getting to, OK? Similar to identity or religion. You gotta dig for it. Please allow me to achieve and convey a degree of significance—even if to a small degree—in a life that, let's say, totally matters.

Yours.

As already stated that it's not feelings motivating me. Not impulses or emotions either. It's your gut, your grit, and maybe even some of your precious time. It boils down to your character. It's that vibe, that truth we project. It's those moments where the shit gets crucial and we are able to affirm to ourselves, "I got this. Okay? I fucking got this." It's a certain balance. A let's-get-real balance of humility and confidence. The extremes—one way or the other, we figure it all out and revel in control of the middle ground we strive to control.

Confidence, not arrogance. It's ambition, not greed, and certainly not at another's expense. Faith over fear. Faith. That's a biggie. Every time. It occurs to me that people more so indoctrinated to faith, through faith, are more likely to uphold certain values and virtues because of their humble acceptance within and of that faith itself. It assumes a value as part of a complete package. Honesty comes to mind. As does one's solemn word.

Let's say, somebody is giving you the big eye and even if for a sec, you are pondering cheating, what you gonna do? Cheat? On your partner? On yourself? Swayed by what? Ass? You're shallow enough to where mere ass can overwhelm you? Well, don't let it. There's your answer. That path renders us cheaters? Liars? WTF. Why be a cheater? Why don't you decide here and now not to cheat? Because Skippy told me not to? No. Because you decide what you're gonna be. And what you're not gonna be. You're gonna do WTF you want to anyway. Why not compel this to be something you'll look back on and be proud of? But I didn't spend a lot of time and a lot of years pondering how to put these words together to entertain degeneracy. Really? Really. Now that you're not a cheater, I submit to you that this jells much better than any brief slice of ass. Some stink-ass at that. Look man. Paging all men. Look at me, yo.

Women go through a lot of bullshit from us. All they pretty much ask for in return from men is kinda basic, really.

"Please be honest with me. Please don't lie to me 'bout the major stuff. Please don't smack me around. And please don't go around boinkin' other women."

We guys are getting a bigtime bargain, you know, and we should be grateful they care enough to give a shit to begin with. How would you wish for a man to treat your daughter one day? You know… lying drains us of energy. Betrays the soul generating your energy. It's a cop-out and simply put, an expression of fear, keeping you trapped and holding you for ransom. There are some feelings for you right there. Be good to our gals. That's all.

And seriously, man, why shit people over money? Why? There's plenty of money out there to be had. Except if you hang out with broke asses. Go make you some coin, earn you some. Just like *r-e-s-p-e-c-t* itself. Nobody owes you nothing, owes you dick. You absolutely must earn respect. If you demand it, guess what? You're an asshole. There's more value in it when you earn it when you create it. And it ain't exclusively for other people. It's for you, your ability, and your face. Stand for you. Represent and relish achievement. You'll live longer. You'll avoid stress, and stress leads to inflammation in your body. The world is a ghetto, but only in a song. We live in the best times man could ever dream of. Let it happen. No pill's gonna cure your ill. Seek remedy from within. Money is a remedy. Not so much may be said of liquor or dope or bales of useless weed bobbing up on sum nameless beach, not from boatloads of fake-ass success, and not from planeloads with gauges all runnin' on empty either. Why do you even need a cure? Hey, here's an idea…try avoiding the disease. Resorting to something guaranteed to destroy and demean you most certainly will. There's the cure. Who says you gotta always be the bullet anyway? Yo, man, try being the gun for a change. Why not give that one a shot? Is your aim true? Are you too much of a dumbass to make a few bucks without stressing anyone out? Why must some of us cause anguish out of resenting others who are able to produce? You can do it too. Maybe we could learn something. If my convict ass can start over and become solvent? Actually creating a job for me and others, for nobody would hire a felon? It's proof and reflects confidence that any dumbass can make it happen likewise. Just ask me.

Let's avoid theft, lies, and manipulations. Avoid cheating, conniving, and deception. Insist your word to matter. I'm a better person for this lifetime of foolishness and ill-conceived antics. For I lived long enough to achieve goodness. Thank goodness. Welcome to Skippy's Church of the Painful Truth, where I can take a few liberties and practically require you to read the shit you might think is boring in order to get to the fun stuff since you have no idea how boring all of that nonsense actually was.

I exist today in amazement that decades later the one thing I garner the most notoriety from is weed. Is flapping weed. What a joke. How pitiful an LOL—Did I just get punked?—joke or what? But if not for the weed-up, there wouldn't be any stage, and wouldn't be any of your attention. Wouldn't be anything for me to write about. Just another Square D tag-along. More pitiful. Wouldn't have been the few million bucks allowing the company with the many unique sorts to search for clues at that very same scene, many of whom have tales to write about also.

Chapter 7
PAGING: All Square Ds

What do you mean? *Square what?* Square Ds, I call 'em. Lemme elaborate. One day we found ourselves at the funeral service of a friend of a friend. The deceased was around eighty-plus when he passed, and I thought to attend the service—even though he wouldn't have attended mine—just out of respect for the guy's friend, who was very near and dear to us and really close to the deceased. There were thirty-three people at this service. We considered that number kinda low, and in fact it was far under the over and under number line I posted prior to the gathering. (That number posted: 67. Ladies and gentlemen, we have a winner. And the under takes it.)

Anyway, the preacher said, "Anyone wishing to say a few words about ole Dave, you may come forward at this time." Nobody budged.

I whispered to my best gal, "No one has anything to say? Nothing? Eighty years, and nobody has anything?"

About then this ole guy stands up, then walks up and begins to speak, opening in eloquence of course by announcing, "I ain't much good at public speaking" (and thanks for the buildup, but anyway).

"Yeah, me and ole Dave worked over there at Square D for forty-three years. Used to go see ole Dave on some weekends and have a cold beer at his house, where he lived for over four decades. Well, adder [after] we worked over there at Square D for thirty years, they threw us a banquet and gave us both a Timex watch. They threw us another banquet adder forty years, and this time they had these two boxes that said Omega on 'em. The presenter said, 'Here's an upgrade; a couple watches for you boys for your long-term dedication to our company for forty years. But before we give 'em to ya, we gotta get those Timexes back.'

I thought the guy was making this up just to have a little something to say. He went on to explain that the company wanted to place the two Timex watches in a showcase on display in their lobby so other employees and customers would have a sense— a reminder—that the company they worked for or might do business with was indeed a reputable and secure organization. And with that, the one speaker sits down, and that's a wrap. Which got me thinking.

That's it? That's this guy's life? Six days later this guy is gone, and it's as if he never existed. The Etch A Sketch has been shaken, people. What? This guy never thought to upgrade his job, house, or significance. Nothing to speak of? Nothing of significance? So now I sorta refer to people in purely exist mode as simply Square Ds. Men and women alike. Most of us simply exist. We get bored and resort to dope, liquor, or affairs to allow us to feel alive. I chose crime because of the rush. Because of that edge. We seek a boost, you know? I see many on our little beach create a purpose to avoid the more common boosters. Save the turtles. Save the homeless dogs. Hug trees. Peel and place Coexist stickers on the bumpers of their Subarus. I did the same thing. Slung some weed. Not much difference at all. And years later some enjoy hearing details of silly boyhood antics. Beats me. BTW, we average three turtle nests every year at our business on the beach at Edisto.

Chapter 8
You Gotta Fight for Your Right

Believe it or not—and this hit me hard—there are tons of people not seeking the company of broke asses, of everyday Square Ds (if you will). Break out the bullhorn and lemme hear ya scream, "Boring." Simply a simple proclamation. The nerve of some people choosing to exercise their precious right to free will. Of association. To have a preference. To simply think as a free person. Hey, I've lived on couches in mobile homes. A few times. Proud of the fact that one was the three-axle variety, to boot. And in contrast, I've lived in many gated communities along with millions of others choosing to do the same. Hey, their preference. My preference too, right? Is this OK? To prefer to live apart and separate from certain elements? Away from a person that my ass absolutely has been a few times, with another shot at it just lurking to swallow up my facade again? As far as I can tell, the path of most Square D types is the path they themselves chose (i.e., we ourselves choose). Exactly as chosen. But not for the long haul. Not this convict. And hey, there is zero ridicule here, OK? Most people are perfectly content to work, to have weekends off, and to not have to bother with running a business. And we totally get it. It's entirely their choice as it was mine not that many years ago. I respect these choices as much as I do yours. Different strokes, man. But this type of lifestyle simply isn't my scene now, nor was it ever. Just wanted to run with the Joneses. Get sucked in by the wretched excesses of life. For one thing I knew not the gratification of other options in life because I lacked the discipline thereby permitting a superficial culture to smother the better judgements. It came at me hard, and rather than strive for the common contentment, Lord, please grant me some avenue to faster wealth. After all, most of us wake up that happy idiot and smuggle for the legal tender. Right? And isn't it our contest with one another to see how much of a chunk we can go and collect? Every day? So what if we choose to trade some security and risk in exchange for a shot at the more instant wealth? Why not. Drug smuggling was that avenue to instant wealth. It showed me shortcuts to achieving wealth. Taught me the mindset of money, and make no mistake, a mindset it becomes. As does the question, at what cost or to what extreme do your limitations allow you—or compel you—to cling to that glory? What if your source is misplaced or dries up? Your great idea becomes obsolete? You get ratted? Or cheated on? Or sick? Or hooked on dope? Outhustled or outsmarted? Your response when loose shit hits the fan defines you. Your worst day. That defines us all. Hey, man, easy is just easy. The time to shine is amid total darkness.

And finding myself indeed mired in Square D mode with jack shit of nothing going on…enough already. Enuf. Whatdoyasay we grab a trick little place in Sea Pines on the south end of Hilton Head? Turns out the attorney from whom we rented the crib was an eventual government snitch boy and was instrumental in the entire *jackpot* investigation coming to be.

But who knew? The poor guy is dead, so no use in painting that window either. Anyway, most others living around me in Sea Pines assumed mine was a familiar story: a single guy working somewhere on the island. Sticks to himself, mows his yard. They would all shit had they known there were a couple bedrooms stuffed full of weed for most of that time. No company, not many visitors, choosing to live in Sea Pines to avoid broke asses who, my assessment was then, were more so inclined to steal my shit. Did I hate anyone? No. Simply exercised the option of free will and the right of association, and like the millions of others choosing the gated community lifestyle, I did not in the least bit give a shit what others might have thought. It's what I think. Cue up my second favorite line in rock 'n' roll: "Doesn't mean that much to me to mean that much to you." And when ya get right down to it, what other people think about me is none of my business. It's their thoughts. Lotta peace to be had there.

Didn't care then; don't care now. The point is that we all have this right to association and to have and exercise our preferences. Should this render hurt feelings or allegations of privilege, FokQ. I give a shit less. But man, oh man...what a great stash house. The best one ever (well, the second-best one). Enclosed garage. Plus, the must-have spacious floor safe already installed.

Therefore, permit me now to redefine my essence minus the stigma of weed. And I do happen to possess essence, you know? Boring as hell, but there's some to be had. However, it doesn't take away from the fact that in the indiscriminate phase of my youth, I chose easy. Chose weed over reason and can't take that back. My kid called me a hypocrite when he was advised by me against the use of weed, and the same advice categorically applies to you, as if you are my own, in that there is no part of me endorsing or condoning stupid. Fall back, my potential friend. Do me the favor and don't read my somewhat contrite little rant in a stoned state. You'll get more out of it. Put the hogglegg down. Resist the twist. And for goodness' sake, people, strangers, and acquaintances alike, stop offering me that shit. And don't come to my grave site one day and flip roaches on me. I'd rather have piss. Have not smoked weed in decades and mostly used to do so to check the quality of the payload in the belly of the boatload. Think of me what you will; I've got a little space to fill. Check it now. People with money prefer not the company of people without. And so you know, I've been broke ass, and I've been not so broke. A few cycles' worth. In one right now. Likely, another to follow. Having wealth allows for more freedom. That's that. Don't make me better; it doesn't elevate me to run some other mode either. The weed experiment taught me how *not* to handle money. Now that there's no weed money to be had, it's far better to learn what not to do with it. And what's the number-one thing not to do with money? Simple. Don't lend any of it out, and don't chill out with broke asses. Not trying to be mean. You were promised real here, not an easy reel. And should the Square D brigade confuse me with someone who gives a shit about what they may think? Swing and a miss. Well…a little white lie there. I care what you think, all right? However, what intrigues me much more is the "why" and the "how" of what you think. Why do we dwell upon what others think anyway? I'd prefer you compete and flourish amid your own thoughts. Couldn't care less what they might be. That's your business.

Chapter 9
How Appropriate, That Number Nine, #9, #9, #9

While the music played, you worked by candlelight. Mom called up to me one night and told me that I had a phone call. I thought, Could it be? Is today the day? The day of an actual smuggling venture? Not merely finding bullshit bales or hustling a few pounds here and there.

"Ahh, hello. Yeah, this is Skippah."

"Hey," a gruff voice called out to me, "go crack the bat." *Click.* which meant proceed to a payphone or the batphone, where presumably there is less likelihood of phone records. Well, be careful what you wish for, son. This was it. The opportunity I had wished for. And with it? Final decision time. All I had to do was do nothing. Say it wasn't a good time. Things just didn't feel right. And that would have been it. No prison. No wasted fifteen years. No gung ho drug agents or prison admin *buffoons* sucking back the

45

wasted public funds on my behalf. Then I could be writing a book instead of admonishing those who ignore laws and take stupid risks. But who wants to read about what they already are? Another boring slug with nothing anyone would wish to review. They call this normal, respected, and civilized life *boring*! I love having achieved boring status for now. Oh, well. But that call? That night? Hopped my ass in the runner bat mobile and batted up.

"It's down in two nights. Thanksgiving night. Be cool. Will be in touch." *Click.*

Celebrate good times; come on. Sure. Many of life's Polaroids flashed on the other side of these lids. Boy Scouts and baseball, my being confirmed in Saint Paul's Episcopal Church in Conway and Saint Helena in Beaufort by a man my mother and grandmother considered their version of Robert Freaking Plant. Bishop Temple was his name. Truly dignified, flowing robes. Keenly cognizant of his image. Regal robes of satin, not cotton, not chintz. A very proud occasion for my mothers, though just a rite of passage that I was compelled to take in order to please those without knowing the gravity of such a path being laid out before me. Many other scenes, times, you know, like in the movie when they flash all the scenes quickly together for a split second. However, other scenes flashed up on my screen too, namely that unforgettable breeze one balmy afternoon down a velvet boulevard, namely a couple microwave ovens I dragged off the beach and stashed in some bushes, and mainly "It's only rock 'n' roll, and I like it." Plus my fourth grade sweetie. Minneree. Now where the hell did that come from? She knew nothing of it. But I knew she would never approve of such antics.

And thus begins my career in the bigger-boy post-up drug game. Eager for action, bring it the %#$^ on. A real-life fantasy is jump-started to life. Hey, I was tired of being broke. OK? That's all. The money thing. I was WTF *t-i-r-e-d* of being broke ass. Why a broke ass? Able to start projects. Unlikely, or more likely as they cried, unable to finish any. Was it me? So easy for some, so easy for most. Seems so useless to have to work so hard, and nothing never really seems to come from it. What piece of the puzzle was lacking here? "Is everything OK, Skippy?" asked the concerned Mommy upon my return from the batphone. Just the wish which was requested. Please. "What's for supper?" Finally, my first off-load was about to actually happen. Batter up.

Chapter 10
The Granny Effect

I did indeed become involved with the culture of weed back in the day. The heyday, we call it—the eighties—from slingin' those mere child's portions of head stash to stacking truckloads of the dreaded contraband to the sky. It was all an engraved invitation to me. Those back-in-the-heydays are behind me now. I ultimately became more and more involved in the weed game and ended up chewing off some prison time as a result. Fifteen and a half years, to be exact. A big, two-time-loser dumbass. That's me. And not so much because what was going down was illegal, you see, but more because I jumped in all this as a non-numbers person. Green. Weed green. No clue as to odds, risk, motives, hustle, or opportunity. On either side. Nothing. Just another slug who likes money and girls—a true foundation for life-altering decisions. Mostly impulsive. The end of the world as we know it. Last summer suddenly.

So why would you want to smuggle weed anyway? I didn't. What's it like? Don't know; didn't care. Can you indeed become that big dumb gorilla walking down your street with pretty women, thereby discovering one may buy into this timely cultural magical misnomer? But remember, once you pull that trigger, the bullet becomes real. Real fast. And oh yeah, suppose it fails, if it should falter, it was not because of inward inadequacies—oh no. It was because of sorry-ass cops, snitches, laws, or bad luck—that blame thing. Blame is indeed an easy way out. Take note of those around you quick to invoke that blame thing. How nice. To some peculiar dumb asses, particularly to the ill-informed like me at the time, the allure of cultlike acceptance tended to deflect those associated risks. And this assumption or justification was thought to somehow compensate for electing to become involved, despite the one-sided odds against it all in the first place.

And with this mindset, I jumped into the arena of illegal drug activity before the majority of life had the opportunity to endear me to its more vital lessons. Make no mistake, there are many that would have become down with the smuggling game had they only been granted the opportunity to jump in. It's a closed society, and so its secret is a closely guarded one, which to the naked eye is all intrigue, connection, and muscle when in truth it's guided by timing and luck, if indeed the term "luck" ought to apply here in the first place. The complexity of all those behind-the-scenes antics seems to be at play. Well, there are none of those things. All of the process was loosely organized, but in my mind, it was quite complex in terms of assumed wealth and clout transitioning to relaxed and real.

I came to refer to the overrating of such matters as "the granny effect."

Once upon a time, my grandmother and mom wanted a new car. So we peeled off a few grand and drove to our fair city of Charleston, where

I visited my ole buddy Eddie and bought them one. A sweet little Honda, back in the eighties. The grandmother was so thrilled about it all, about my precious time allotted to them that you would have thought I personally designed and manufactured the components and actually assembled the damn thing in her front yard. All I did was go drive one home. Thank you, Eddie. Precious time. Indeed.

Chapter 11
Let's Rat Lawyers in Love

Speaking of the granny effect, here's another superb example. Years after the fact, once people decided to write about what went down, there was occasion to view a couple interviews with the Jackpot prosecutors. And they'd go on about how we "gentlemen smugglers" were some of the most crafty, elusive and logistical experts in the world. Begging the question in my mind, "Who the hell are they talking about—us?" Yeah. They were. Their vibe was to put forth a narrative that we were extremely difficult to identify and pursue. We had the ultimate discipline and experts in the various fields. A total bunch of bullshit. We were disorganized to no end. The big time Colombian connections were local Mestizos coming out to meet our mother boats in canoes. Tossing bales on the deck, which were weighed by a guy standing on a bathroom scale. The Feds wanted to merely project themselves as supersharp guys able to "crack the codes" or some such BS as this. The real deal was this: most drug agents and fed people—while worlds more capable than state and local actors—are driven by results. First they had to establish the dire consequences of the subject pursuit in order to justify the need for their agency to begin with. They live pretty much a boring, broke, Square D life to begin with, so it's easy for them to use class envy as a motivator. And this is the strategy. Still. Next comes creating snitch boys. Let's face it. Without snitch bitches, they have nothing. Still.

Subsequently comes the passing of conspiracy statutes allow hearsay evidence if it is from a coconspirator. They then indict pot smokers who are scared to death and say whatever prosecutors demand they spew in exchange for nol-prossed or lesser-included guilty pleas (the same thing). The prosecutors then post up on TV, posing with a few pounds of weed and a stack of twenties they split up later. Use the confiscated weed to set up further snitches. Use the money to chase skinny girls, giving the fat ass wives a break. What about entrapment, you say? There is no entrapment. Or any other color of law defect once the target pleads guilty or nolls up. All such defects or strategies by any/all arms of government vanquished.

I've seen firsthand cases where drug agencies supplied both the money to buy and the dope to facilitate the deal. To create snitch boys. And guess what? The guys involved on the wrong end made the deal out to be a setup and kept both the dope and the cash. One sterling never-told story. Sure, 100 percent entrapment, *unless* and until the subject pleads guilty, which 99 percent do (which both agencies fully expect as forthcoming—ruh-roh, Astro). They had free rein, for all the money and dope were stolen to begin with.

Again, once guilty pleas or the more bullshit nolo contendere pleas are entered, any and all color of law defects to this point are absolutely absolved. Now there's some dry snitchin' for ya. I tell you this because no attorney will ever, not ever, mention this to ya. That it's the driving force in a multibillion-dollar hustle. For mainly their hustle is to attack the freshly indicted defendant, size them up foremost regarding primarily their perceived ability to pay. Barking out to family members how they gonna get their best guys on this shit, for "we feel the defendant has been wronged. We'll need X amount by tomorrow a.m., and we'll have the guy out on bond by tomorrow night."

Once your family hands them that initial impulsive chunk? That's a wrap my friend. Bank that. The lawyer's focus typically shifts, and he's off to feed upon other such hopeful mullets. The new focus is to encourage and allow the guilty plea to run its course. Why? you ask. That's easy too, people. Once a guilty plea is entered, they are allowed to keep any and all money they sucked out of you. End of fucking story. And end of story from a non lawyer slug, OK? This is merely from situations I've witnessed. Not anything remotely suggesting you to act upon. That would be a matter for you and a real attorney. But for now don't say nobody ever gave a shit enough to tell you.

Its rarely any significant follow through afterwards to be had, investigative-wise or otherwise. They are protected from any reimbursement of initial monies received through the 99-percent-likely guilty plea celebrations once accepted.

We had zero clue during the hey days what we were doing. With emphasis. Running blind and running hard. Shocked we didn't get made sooner.

Chapter 12
First Cane Pearly Gate, Big Fish

To me, many people seem to break their flappin' necks to come across as "nice," as if somehow "nice" is construed as smart, educated, and disciplined. I find it difficult to take a man seriously, for example, when he refers to this world's buckets of shit as simply "folks" or uses for terms of emphatic measure such endearing words as "gosh" or "golly" even when certain "folks" reveal their true character as disingenuous. I remember in the big house, all the duty guards (COs) were trained to refer to all of us inmates as "gentlemen." What a crock. The majority of the so-called "gentlemen" were nothing more than a collective group of deranged pervs amid a larger segment of deranged pervs genuinely believing they were the subject of every woman's (CO's) fantasy, when the majority of such women were under an unrelenting threat of being "tree jumped" (Basically raped. Prison smack where a guy climbs a tree and waits for some unsuspecting little anybody to walk by.). Very few female COs realize the dangers they faced on a daily basis. Here's a profound opinion: women have no business being subjected to the coarse environment being a men's prison guard has to offer. There's your gentlemen of the penitentiary sort ever so needful to project the tough guy image. The "don't fcuk with me in here" guy. Quite contrary to the Gentlemen Smugglers at hand, attempting to live up and prop up an opposite image as the "misread" or the "why'd they come after me?" guy.

My advice to anybody longing for the drug game is to rethink it. Especially weed. The deck is stacked. Avoid. It is indeed a "gateway" drug, not so much in the physical capacity, more absolutely in the capacity of an acceptance of other, more dangerous decisions. I refer you to one innocent glide down the beach one balmy summer day in a convertible velvet Caddy. Weed is also dangerous, to boot. People told me to rethink my option all the time as I weighed the pros and cons of drug involvement. Listen, when people you know demonstrate they actually care about you and attempt to extend to you some advice on any given topic, at least take a few minutes to analyze what they have to say. And imagine a world where no one giving a rat's ass enough to even pretend to care. Furthermore, acknowledge gratitude, even if only to yourself; there are indeed people in your life who truly give a shit. And there's a lot said there to be grateful for.

Rethink it, kid, OK? Because I was too chickenshit to grab the creature by the horns, I figured to check out pending degrees of involvement instead, to a lesser degree of inclusion. You see, my family had a place so terribly suitable for unloading the boatloads of contraband. So I figured to discover guys who could hook us up with other guys seeking a prime spot in which to unload the many boatloads of weed coming in already at the time.

There's a lot of illusion that comes with drug smuggling, so I thought to employ the "granny effect" with the notion I was never gonna be down at the off-load site personally. As if Mr. Mysterious had come to freakin' town. I played it off and remembered the quote my granddad told me: The rules of plantation ownership are that when you do happen to own the plantation, don't work on it. As if to say, keep your distance from you and the ones that do work in the place so as not to spoil the elevated perception they may quite naturally classify you under. Hoping you are stable. Hoping your and their jobs are secure. Be careful whom you let into your house too. Your house is more than where you live, you know. It's your head; it's your very space itself. It's your mind, and it's up to you to set it in place. Ever see a pro football player on the roster sittin' in the owner's box? Very, very seldom. Owners are producers, and to mingle with employees carries zero advantage to owners personally. What if you have to shit can them one day? What if your kids boinkin' one of 'em? Just the way of the world. A different class, a different mindset. It's simply part of the illusion of wealth, intrigue, and even intellect. Therefore getting out there and slingin' bales with the off loaders sorta takes away some of the structure and due course of that ownership and of the illusion therein assumed. Image, baby. I'm certain everyone "granny effects" intrigue and organization into various aspects of their own lives as they submit the presentations. When we're young, when we don't know better, and our gullible audience sorta sits there waiting to applaud, when they do…what the hell? Take a bow.

Our offload place was a large farm. "The spot," we called it. I called it. It used to be a working plantation, and my ancestors became quite wealthy growing the cotton. They smuggled a little liquor during Prohibition. So what? Tell me...so what if you have a history of a particular place? Your people have owned it for a long time. While I do suppose this demonstrates prior generations had enough hustle and enough moxie in them to be able to hang on to the property for a while, it seems to me that some people without such history place a little bit more value in its overall interpretation as possessing a bit more clout than it actually does. Don't misconstrue the bottom line: I'm very grateful they were able to pull it off. Able to enjoy a life, perhaps even a significant life, having the foresight to leave a little something for those that may follow. I am a fortunate son in that, amid the right to exist in a time in which I may choose to be a significant player in the shadows of my ancestors, I feel the grandest obligation and tribute to them is to demonstrate that same capacity to not just live for this ego's end run. So that they do not make the many sacrifices merely for my consumption and for me to vacate the scene with no deposit and no return for those who follow.

However, it nonetheless doesn't guarantee that place or that property in your possession forever, does it? 'Course not. We happen to have property that's been in the family for a couple centuries. Just like the name. Is your history the value of the name in your life? Or is it the value of you—your face, your character? Does it matter a rat's ass whether your grandpa lived in some town or another for a few decades or not? That was then, and that was their gig. What's yours? Surely you've heard people, when prompted and finding themselves in a fix, with not much of a clever response or defense at hand, default to "Do you know who I am? Do you have any idea who you're dealing with here?" Well, no, actually, who the fcuk are you again? Since you ask, this ain't no ID check, MF, but rather a concern involving someone obviously assuming his name, his money, or his history should allow a privileged consideration to enter the equation as an expected and higher regarded third party. How is this even relevant? Isn't the issue, discussion, or conflict between the two parties at hand? Might we simply address one another here as two people, two equals, hashing out some detail or another? Personally, yours truly chooses to forgo any assumed edge, that unique prestige if you will, due to past family members. That was them. Wasn't me. There are several business people in my world curious about that decision, for they believe the mystique of yesteryear itself would either boost my own credibility—a convicted felon could use a dose of that, no doubt—or allow those on the receiving end a true connection to such a heritage, which they might come to relish, so as to reinforce their social prowess, certainly worthy of the affiliation. Shit. It just hit me, y'all. Really. Perhaps I don't place a lot of value in my own history because of recognizing there wouldn't be any value contributing to the overall perception of somebody else's intrigue.

As it began to dawn upon me that our farm was being used as a weed off-load destination, I sought to become introduced in the drug world to somebody in the market for a place to unload a boatload or twenty—someone other than the DEA, that is. The DEA used the place several times that I'm aware of, as was revealed during federal Jackpot smuggling trial number one (83-165). And this was the main reason my acquittal by the jury at that trial the first time around.

But prior to the next level of weed smuggling involvement up in South Carolina, a few trips to Florida, where most of the weed was coming in at the time, were taken. Eager for action and hot for the game, it was easy to meet a seller of weed and establish a connection. My first score from Fort Lauderdale was a score of four pounds. In a VW bus as the runner machine. My first connection was through a guy named Ray and his most gorgeous girlfriend, named Kayne. OMG. Poor me… a sparkling glass of red, would ya please?

Among the continuing figuring out of life's discovery back then, smacked me at point-blank range just why men of means typically prefer these better looking types of women. As a couple Eagles so eloquently delivered to us in one of the more splendid opening lines ever; 'City girls just seem to find out early how to open doors with just a smile.' How true. Seems the better looking ones tend to be invited by these men of means to other places and countries. They experience other cultures, and as such are rendered a bit more diverse and refined through the process. They're more well-rounded, better mannered, and know more about the proper etiquette. Poise. Etiquette. They're more readily able to dial in these attributes. The finer things for them become everyday measures of self-imposed standards. And the biggie for me—they learn how to properly hold a fork and knife when out at a higher-end establishment (keep the hands low, my dear, OK?). It's embarrassing to me when I'm in the company of anyone holding their utensils like they're in the flappin' penitentiary, standing guard over a piece of cheap meat. Bottom line?

Larger babes aren't perceived as smart or as educated as smaller ones (emphasis on the word "perceived" here). And are typically moved around more frequently by Greyhound buses than by Delta jets. Just telling ya what I've observed. Truth is truth. Just conveying it. And the reason? Here's another firsthand opinion. Guys with more discretionary means seem a bit more selective when it gets down to it. Why do you think we pursue this—our version of happiness? After all, we're the ones issuing the invites. I mean, you wouldn't wish to deny anyone his or her right to preference, would you? Of course not. But the real danger here is that some gals take this personally and begin to resent this right to preference itself. And success. Or just plain men in general. Then may ensue feelings of inadequacy. Of loneliness. Blaming others. And next may appear bouts of rebellion toward us. Toward those making any such lavish lifestyle possible through innovation, intellect, and contribution.

Throughout our history, women in general have been a huge motivator. Wouldn't you agree? Hey, there wouldn't be much creativity if not for the rewarding company and complement of a woman. There damn sure wouldn't be any rock 'n' roll. Imagine a world without Jackson Browne. Shudder to think.

Please don't rebel. Collecting pets to feel needed? Resorting to alcohol, dope, or both or adapting the habit to gradually eating more of the wrong foods (i.e., sugars and carbs), all the while blaming it on "assholes" like me 'cause you were left off the flight log to Saint Croix? Please. But again, simply observing here. No ridicule. If you're a larger person and comfortable with your weight, that's on you (there's an unintended pun for ya). However, might we ask the more relevant question: Wouldn't you rather be comfortable with your health instead? With the odds and chances better setting you up for fulfillment?

Do you perhaps stuff your face at fast-food places more than you should? Here's some advice and a good place to start. Try cutting back on this one. Your health will thank you for it. And lottery tickets. Why? Why is this a primary element of your retirement strategy? Only you know the answer. Avoid being played. That's all. It's what you're eating. It's what you allow in your headset. Educate yourself. It ain't that difficult, you know. Food companies make more money selling you mostly carbohydrates and sugars. And states make more money when you purchase more, not fewer, lottery tickets. Become informed enough to know why you shouldn't. You gotta start somewhere. You're already smart enough. Read it, now. You're already smart enough. Get comfortable with that. Invest in that which you possess above the neck as it's by design destined to grow your entire life. Unlike the physical, the vanity, and all those other worldly distractions, the main one above the neck sticks with you for life. And compliments you more so as you age, far above those misguided whims of vanity and delight.

My wish for you is success and contentment. Seriously. You know why they call it a mindset? Easy. Because it's your mind, and you're 100 percent in charge of setting it. Get out of the way and let it happen. Betcha, by golly, wow, you've accomplished far more difficult things in your life. Take some time. You have life. Simply add a sprinkle of living to it. And listen to this: if my convict, criminal, broke, half-dead, no-skills, goofy ass can make a decent run at it, you got this too. Just sayin.'

So anyway, back to this connection with Kayne, who incidentally was not one of the aprons having my number on the wall; she worked in a very large record store in Fort Lauderdale called Peaches. The store was probably fifteen-to-twenty-thousand square feet, back when vinyl record albums were a big deal. At the time, huge musical acts frequented Fort Lauderdale. As the rhythm of these runs to Fort Lauderdale matured, so did sorta hangin' out at Peaches Records while this gal's boyfriend, ole Raymond, stepped out and about on his turf trying to scrounge up my next order. On one of these later trips, Kayne said she had been hired to throw a large party in sort of a concierge capacity for a visiting national touring act and was in charge of putting on one of those talk-of-the-town-hype throw downs. She asked if I could make the run to the liquor store and deliver back the necessities for the party. Off to the liquor store breezes little ole goofy-ass me to pick up her called-in order, and upon showing up there and saying, "Kayne sent me," I was from then on treated like the big shot she was.

During the loading process of the beer and liquor into my weed runner VW bus with a hand truck provided by the liquor store, there was an introduction. While I was bringing the third and final stack of goodies out to the van, the Hell's Angel guy who apparently owned the liquor store slipped me a small vial. "Here ya go, dude, a little something for the effort."

What the hell is this? About two or three inches long, with a small faucet-type lever on one end. Had never seen this before and had no idea what it was or what to do with it. Was it part of the delivery? Didn't know. Hell…I'm from Beaufort, South Carolina, cuz. Plus, I've never ever been referred to as "dude" either. WTF is a dude, anyway? As in, "Any major dude will tell you, my friend"?

And, people, just off topic a bit, at Beaufort High, there were many Marines' kids attending. This particular very beautiful girl was from the Far East, presumably stationed there with the family. One day she referred to a group of us simply as "people." Whoa. I'd not ever been called "people." Was more used to being referred to as "y'all." Freaked me out a little. And now this guy calls me "dude." 'People' turns out to be pretty cool. But this dude thing...

Anyway, I unloaded the last hand truck of supplies into the ole trusty VW bus, took the hand truck back up onto the curb, hopped in the van, and proceeded with my return trip to the party venue with all the goodies.

Several miles down the road, up rolls a quite irate liquor store owner on a Harley, demanding, "Let's pull it over, pal." It dawned on me immediately: Oh shit, was I supposed to pay for all this? Kayne sorta implied it was a simple delivery on my part and said, "to remember to bring the ticket" and she would pay for it later during the party. But no, it wasn't about any of this.

The guy said, "Hey, asshole, where is my shit?" to which I replied, "What are you talking about?" He said he wanted his "bullet" back and that there was three hundred dollars' worth of blow in there. And I thought, Oh, he must be talking about that little vial he slipped me.

"Oh, you mean this, this thing right here?" At which point I produced the vial, saying sorry, but I thought that it was a gift, a tip, or part of the delivery back to Kayne.

He said, "No, stupid shit, it's nose candy."

"What? What do you mean? What?"

"Your country ass doesn't know what this is?"

"I guess not."

About this time the guy begins to recognize that there is indeed a void in my mind as to any idea what this scene—this street scene—is about, and he says to me, "Gimme the damn thing."

He pops it on his palm a couple of times and says, "Here, stupid ass, take you a whiff-of-jiff," which I did as he snatched the thing back through his outstretched hand, snapping his fingers, saying, "Here you go, Einstein, this is a little jolt for the other side." And with that he rode off on his Harley, rolling his eyes at my lack of street real. (One doesn't drive a Harley either. It's a ride, as opposed to a drive. Learned that one too.).

And there you have the short version of my introduction to and indoctrination into the world of cocaine. I was flying like a bird. She don't lie, she don't lie, she don't lie, cocaine. Not quite the fantasy introduction, as was the case with the first weed the people.

Turns out this dude guy was at the fabulous party that night and introduced me, along with the amusing story earlier that afternoon, to his wife. They handed me the very same vial, kinda snickering. "You know what this is, right?"

Oh yeah. Who am I foolin'? I started following the guy around like a personal butler. Later on, as the night began running a little hot, I could barely see the road for the heat coming off it, and "dude" eased up a bit. "I gotta feeling you'll remember me, and I guess we should have welcomed you a bit more graciously to our piece of paradise of state number twenty-seven." It pleased me to see some civility in the mix.

Please indulge me here; for the first time, doing some blast has little value in anyone's eyes, not to mention it is the ultimate boring loser story. It's only included as an occasion to present this liquor store owner's "theme," if you will. He considered the drug a "thanks for the business" gesture while simultaneously imparting some weathered wisdom for my consumption, which seemed to invite caution to a degree amid this, my next step in the drug culture in general; I remember like yesterday his parting shot:

"Always the bullet, never the gun; always the lover, never the one."

"Nice meetin' ya, dude." There's a boatload of possibility in that last line he passed on to me. It was indeed a warning to the wise regarding this more powerful narcotic. As if. The bullet has no direction you see. A gun is required to direct it. All day. But wait. He who controls the gun? Controls direction of the bullet. Pick one if you must. Proceed with caution. You better. This man was a weathered Hell's Angel business member. And had no doubt lived an underworld life as few of us can even imagine. He'd seen the perils of drug usage over decades of life and through it all offered up this warning label to me. And you know what? Every single time I brought a straw or rolled up hundred-dollar bill close to my beak, this man's image would appear. Would find myself in situations where needles were around, and simply said, "No. Not for me." Thank you Nancy. Thank you my Angel. Coulda been worse. Just for what its worth.

But anyway, back to that first four-pound run from Florida. My ass was so stressed there was gonna be a drug bust upon my return to Beaufort, South Carolina, that I actually pulled over in my buddy's Mercury Outboard dealership yard just past the Broad River Bridge in total surrender with hands literally in the air simply due to a car sorta tailgating and heading my same way up from Savannah. Scary ass. When the car continued on by, whny, there stood dummy gummy me completely baffled (and wondering a bit these years later what they could have been thinking). How could someone haul weed around and no one know? Man, maybe my ass ain't built for this gig...all the way from Florida? Slough it off to driver's fatigue?

Oh, how could it be that no one knew? Easy. Because I did not tell anyone. That's how. From that flashbulb, on and upon being extremely embarrassed by myself, the practice and the discipline of not telling just anyone any nonsensical clutter they did not need to know (present effort not withstanding) emerged. And it is due to this discipline that it may be stated that never once—as in never *o-n-c-e*—did a bust go down with anything on my person. Not any of the fifty tons of weed I hauled around, not any of the millions in cash being transported all over the place, not any other type of contraband, assets, toys, nothing. And not any weapons either.

Didn't carry any. Wasn't in our world. Oh, there were some close calls along the way; don't get me wrong. It's easy. Keep your shit together, pay attention to what's surrounding you, and never drive around smoking weed as a surprising number of druggies do and are shocked when they are busted. When I was not hauling any goodies, there were several occasions when the police would flash blue lights in my direction. Quickly. Make that split decision. Sometimes the option was exercised. Gear it down a notch or two and stomp that petal on the right. Do the math. Figure the odds. If you are already rolling triple digits or close to it and blue is approaching and clocking you? Fcuk it. Kick it in. Fan the brakes as if you are slowing to pull over while running it up to a buck-twenty. You would travel one mile every thirty seconds that way. Meanwhile, our guy in blue is faced with the tedious task of braking, turning around, and accelerating back to highway speeds in order to give you a run. By this time? You should be a couple miles away and out of sight. Pursuit over. Only at night. Only on back roads. Those were stupid times for me. Regret abounds for needlessly placing others at risk. No more. Don't you even consider such dumb ass moves, OK? Promise me.

A short time after some harrowing runs, a notification from a buddy connected to him to "meet the man" in Columbia, South Carolina came my way. Enough of these small town clown hustles. When I spoke to the guy, he said, "How 'bout tomorrow for lunch at a place called Yesterdays in Five Points?" Sure thing. So off to Cola Town, my ass rumbles. Once there, having rolled up to Yesterday's, I was summoned over to a table and met my first kingpin. Flash. Very cool. Pretty girl with him and everything. Both sportin' his 'n' hers big fat gold Rolex watches. Hell, up until that instant, my ass thought Rolex was referring to a brand of scuba-diving equipment, talking about how it's good to 120 feet and all.

Anyway, the deal with me was laid out quickly and in pretty simple terms: "We've used your place down there at Edisto for some time now and will continue to use it. However, there are of late many others using it, and it's getting rather cramped on ole Off-Load Lane. With me? If you boys were to throw up a gate there and give me the exclusive, you could expect to make a million or so per year. Should we yap further? Or you want the Yesterday's meat and three veggies special? The meatloaf is killer."

"No."

It ain't every day one has the occasion to meet a kingpin. We are talking about a real kingpin. Well, one was met that day. Flash. I'd heard about the guy. Sorta an elusive-type guy. Not too quick to allow others into his circle. His house. He allowed me in it due to the fact that there was a connection to a really superb off-load site for the many payloads of weed he was directing up this way. Gotta have an off-load site, people. Easy enough.

OK. In the scheme of things at the time, Flash was what we street people referred to as a "Big Fish." The "Big Fish." For comparison, those like me were tagged with a slightly different moniker. Yeah. Mine was more along the lines of "mullet breath." Meandering around in a ditch somewhere. Me no "Big Fish." Not by a long shot. There's the NFL; then there's Pop Warner. Are you with me? There's mullet, and there's marlin. Blue marlin, baby. The marlin is the big fish for real. Think about the marlin and what makes them known worldwide as the ultimate reel-in, the ultimate real "big fish."

The blue marlin is—without question—the most coveted prize in the fishing world. Period. Starting with the dozens of huge companies that produce multimillion-dollar sport fishers whose main pursuit is to reel in these magnificent specimens. Then there are the people who design and build these huge sport boats. Thousands and thousands of 'em. There are an additional tens of thousands of people crewing these vessels worldwide. Thousands more are building marinas where hundreds of thousands of sport fishers can tie up. The fuel, equipment. The electronics. The tournaments. The jets are flying people all over the world to avail themselves to various tournaments. The hotels. The entertainment. All for that rare instant when the special Marlin Flag is able to be hoisted upon the grand prize reeled in. Might we dare suggest a trillion-dollar industry? Billions more every year. And for what? you ask. For that "big fish," baby. For that Flash of the cotton-pickin' oceans. There ain't no next step above the pinnacle, people. The marlin is it.

As for me that day, meeting Flash? This analogy parallels my sentiments in exact terms upon gaining access to and meeting this guy. My arrival came to fruition face-to-face and eye-to-eye. The ocean's grandest prize. Right before my eyes. Breathing the same air. King air. My ass wished to smuggle weed. Ain't no next step up feasible in our world as known by me. This is it. For opportunity? Wanting a crack at it? Careful. He just showed up. The ball is in my court now. Finally. And sure. He could wiggle amid that "granny effect" some. Maybe more than some. Didn't matter. Bottom line, this cat had the moxie to pull it off. To get the hell out of the way and let that shit just happen. OK? He's on record later, having proclaimed, "It ain't for everybody." He's dead on. Hey, anybody can do it, but ain't just anybody able to pull it off. It ain't for everybody. It was for Flash. He has that "it" factor. Hell, he invented it, wrote it, and then lived it. Nobody needs to ask if he wants his window painted. As for me? There is no excuse to throttle back any further.

About now, I'd be remiss to omit another Kingpin my having been apprised of during our Jackpot trials, but only coming to meet him more recently. He came up with one compelling line when prompted, "Why didn't you rat? You have a whopping 182 witnesses against you and still, you remain steadfastly pure of your decision not to snitch. What gives?"

His response? "It's simply not in my DNA. Next question."

Hey dudes. Hey people. This man is Les Riley. And one strong MF. Hats off.

OK, back to other less significant events never to be forgotten either. "Paging: two bales on the beach. Come in, London. One small step for man—one giant leap...gee, 'I wish that I had Jesse's girl.'" Mine was a laser beam of stroke. A basket of clout, of focus falls from the sky as officially delivering uDam as in the rick. As of now, I ain't showin' up anymore, MF; I'll be arriving, thank you very much. Seems so useless to have to work so hard, and nothing ever really seems to come of it. Seems we heard that one prior.

Needless to say, it was on. But then? Had to embarrass myself in front of Flash and come clean, "I have no money. Running on MT. It would take me a while to handle this gate thing. When it's ready, you'll get a call."

Then Flash said, "Let's take a walk." We proceeded outside and up toward a beautiful new burgundy BMW 733i. Flash told me to get in. "Keys and paperwork in the glove box; call me when there's a gate." I snagged the envelope out of the glove and started back to my piece-of-junked-up truck to go stash it. He said, "Leave the papers with the car. Take the car. You can't have the car, but you may use it as a gesture of sincerity. And the eight grand, and the little surprise? Welcome to the rock."

Twenty minutes later I'm breezing down I-26 east toward home. Naturally the Bimmer came with an Escort hardwired. This was the time when radar detectors were first introduced to the driving public. The same company that sold the police radars sold radar detectors to us, the much larger consumer base. They were at that time the absolute ticket to ride. Can't drive fifty-five. And the Bimmer? Tricked. Five-speed. Scalded-dog-ass fast. Such a fine glide at eighty-five. A jammin' after-market Blaupunkt system. Not to mention the eight grand riding shotgun welcoming me to the headliner's slot. And the surprise? Why, it was a little child's portion of the cocaine for the membrane. For the membrane, he cries. No pissed-off biker demanding to pull it over this time. Didn't do any. Never sucked back a line alone. No one to yap to.

We called it blast. A few jolts. Good to go. Yep. Skippy did indeed suck back a few beakfulls of blast-for-me in my time. What? Should I chew off another ten years? That cleans my slate? Shave my ass with a straight razor? OK? Decree whatever degree of "dignity" the state might discern or be deprived of, which may have been violated? Or you. What do say you? FM. I'll suck it back if I jolly damn well want to, so get the fokQ over it. I'd ten times rather do blast than weed or pop all these fcuking pills everyone inhales these days, going around counting boring-ass turtle nests, believing they suddenly swim with purpose and significance. "But a doctor prescribed them." Horseshit. Still a druggie. And I'd a hundred times rather not do any of this shit, which is now my choice going forward. Choosing not to partake in any of it, just so you know. "Any of it," he cries. Not because it may be illegal, mind you. And certainly not because some fat ass judge or law somewhere says, "Hey, man, you shouldn't do that either." Wouldn't give a shit if it's legal or not. My choice—it's my gigantic beak. As it is now my choice not to partake, exactly as it was then to opt in; it's the same these times to no-go. Been there. Sucked it back. Decided one day...that's a wrap. Opted out. It's my business. Kiss my skinny, nonevolved monkey white ass. That's WTF you can do. The end.

Besides, my current ongoing best gal and last gal keep me in line. Another kinda of line much preferred. Cocaine is meant to be done in good company. For the record my belief is that weed is far more dangerous than blast. Eventually everybody gets through their blast phase, and most move on to have a life. Either that, or they typically end up flappin' broke, locked up, and/or dead. Weed tends to hold on to more strongly to ya the longer its use continues, and much of its allure is due to the fact most of us think it's harmless. It ain't. Cocaine, alcohol, and legal dope are similar in their breakdown as they're water-soluble, unlike weed, which is more broken down over time and stored in fatty tissue. Takes longer for organs to get rid of it. Livers and kidneys clean one's water-soluble toxins out of the body much faster than they do weed. Weed lingers around for a month or so, and when you keep piling it on, its user is basically rendered poisoned. Just one man's opinion? Most legal drugs are designed to be flushed quickly, requiring users to replenish the source frequently, therefore benefiting the drug makers. The dope sellers. Just an observation.

On the way back from Cola, I swing into Walterboro and purchase gate-building necessities. Everything but the posts. Hit the drawbridge to our beloved Edisto Island around six that evening. You know what it's like to have not much more than one minute, then six hours later suddenly mediocrity has a little spunk? Has a little fire? My crusty ass hit the island in a new Bimmer, a nice wad of Benjies in the pocket, geeked up, and beaked up with a cute little sack of yapalot. Mom and Granny were in Beaufort during the week at this time. So I stopped by the house and decided to venture out that night. Most folks around Edisto applied the "granny effect" to us all our lives, so there wasn't too much terrible concern with flaunting the windfall. No one knew anything. Only what I told 'em, which was "Hey, come see what's it like to glide with the chosen few; gotta surprise for ya."

Here's the truest line of this book. That gate? That Flash demanded? That gate was the fastest gate erected in the history of mankind. By nine o'clock the next morning, it was done. A pretty nice gate at that. It was not only a gate to our place, to our privacy, and to opportunity itself; to me, it represented the open door to the possibility of wealth. Real wealth. The kind my ancestors may have known. The kind in total elude mode to me. Zero concept of. So foreign and distant and only intended for others. What's your name? Whose your daddy? Is he rich like me?

Flash was contacted, and it was back to Cola town. Back in Columbia, the confession came out to Flash that the gate only cost around six hundred bucks. He said keep the change, keep the sack, but gimme back my ride. Hey, this works. A month later came that first independent off-load, and for that, the wish finally came true that this boy had indeed arrived, baby.

Chapter 13
Simply L

My local boy "L" had set that first off-load up and came through with forty thousand a couple weeks later. Forty thousand from zero cash one day to forty thousand the next. Imagine this with me for a minute or two if you would. Forty large this day. Zip large the previous day. "L" was my classmate in high school. He willed this type of deal to happen. I couldn't match his determination, mainly 'cause it wasn't this critical to me. He had no backup. He had no (assumed) trust fund. He had no wealthy first cousin Syd to dial up. He's appreciated all the more, though, for this moxie. If not for his consistency, there wouldn't have been these recollections. He passed away recently due to steroid use during his legit attempt to become a pro tennis player in his youth. It caused him severe inflammation in his fifties. And he's gone. He sat on that defense bench with us during the jackpot trials. There ain't many sons of bitches I can say this about. He didn't take any shit and valued his words as truth. Convenience, be damned. Sure, we could have, and dare I state, should have, channeled our energies elsewhere. But we didn't. It was what it was, and it is what it is. There're still a few guys to lean on with his grit. Those few I can count on one flappin' hand. We might refer to those four fingers of reliability as our own Mt. Rushmore. We all have it. Wish that you might know a man like Larry McCall. That's all. Covers your action and goes you one more.

The first off-load came to be one Thanksgiving night. It was the ultimate rush. Much the same vibe as placing a large bet on a football game. All-or-nothing proposition. It was a bit chilly, I remember. Just hangin' out at my grandmother's house across the way from the off-load spot. Darkness arrived rather early, and when dear ole Mom called me to supper, I couldn't eat. Couldn't tell her what was going down. I heard slight commotions over at the spot, and when I ventured out into the yard and peered through the night vision equipment provided, I couldn't see any movement down by the river. It started getting on toward nine, then ten o'clock…nothing. Naturally I presumed the worst had occurred and the boat had been busted. 'Course, it hadn't. A little bit later, I was praying the boat would be busted before it made it to our place, for surely it would be busted here. Then came the mild flashback to the times I drove back a few pounds from Florida. Remember? How paranoid was I? I chilled and thought, Hey, if it's busted, then it's busted. But hell, I hadn't told anyone. Didn't know the actual off-loaders. Didn't know what type of boat it was, much less any of the guys on it. So I went inside and sipped a nightcap glass of sherry with Mother (the same brand of sherry is used by the Episcopal Church, as related to my grandmother by none other than the much revered Bishop Temple himself). Then about midnight I heard yapping and load engines idling, pushing, and keeping the boat against the mud bank as there was no dock as such. Just a small bluff of mud. Let me tell you, how deathly quiet that place can become at dead low tide with absolutely zero wind. Freakishly so.

But here we are. Me at the spot that next morning after the first off-load, looking over the ground by the riverbank, littered with around forty pounds of unclaimed weed spillage. The weed had escaped from busted-up bales hastily tossed down from a shrimp boat bumped up against the riverbank, and then the precious cargo was placed on rental trucks and rolled off the property early the next morning. Never mind the matted-down grass, the huge hull print left behind in the mud, the truck tire tracks longing to get the hell outta there—none of that. I'd not consumed weed on a regular basis at this point but gathered the forty-pound escapees up in a couple large garbage bags and proceeded to drop it off with Julio down by the schoolyard a few miles away and to some black dudes playing basketball. Years later dudes would confide in me that those bags of weed stayed there for a few hours undisturbed 'cause they all thought it had to be a setup.

Chapter 14
More Fun, More Funding

Let's go blue light specials. Here's my take on law enforcement in general versus the few individual officers in particular. Government is necessary, as is law enforcement. Additionally, law enforcement officers—LEOs—single-handedly allow the government itself to exist. Law enforcement allows the flexibility of the government to be possible. Allows us self-determination, as in the right to vote, associate, own property, hell, even freedom itself, as I see it. In this fcuked-up world where many of us the people seem to thrive, many of us have become so expectant of civility and process that we tend to simply ignore the value of liberty. And in so doing, we perhaps unknowingly exchange a bit of critical awareness for somebody else's free shit promised to us through politicians able to buy our votes. Not that it matters necessarily how we vote, but more so who counts the votes.

In our choice to wonder around stoned, to waste away in Margaritaville, to obsess about sports or how much other people earn—these useless pastimes transition us to mere useful idiots. Look around. We have inadvertently created a dependent society. By a dependent society, I simply mean a class of weed the people totally built and enslaved through entitlements. Boosted up through resentment and divisiveness. This boost is achieved by indoctrinating the masses whereby equal opportunity should and must translate in real time to equal results. This concept is fcuking lunacy. Wait a minute, not so fast: Where do you think we stack 100 percent of the responsibility for controlling these types out and about running free among us? Expecting our free shit. Resentful of the idea, we've had it too good for too long. Right again, Batman. At our doorstep, opposing such antics, are law enforcement officers. The evil brainwashing of those more susceptible to an escape, a remedy, or some sort of hope, if you will, once transitioned into the contagious malignant mindset it has assumed, seem to excuse crime. Excuse theft. Excuse addictions. The longer this trend continues and the more extreme it becomes, the more we, as producers, as one-time independent, self-reliant souls, shall come to discover our reliance upon law enforcement to control this insanity. Granting passage back to some order. These everyday people, as we have witnessed, become inhibited via this same tortuous strategy. And who do we rely upon to contend with such political ebbs and flows? You better ask somebody, homeboy.

And here's a little nugget for all you druggies slingin' it and bringin' it, all biatched up about how cops always seem to be "in your way." Check it now. Reach for the real.

If not for cops? First off, what permits illegal dope to have value to begin with? Hello. It's law enforcement. Druggies are paid to run the gauntlet; we are paid to confront the risk. A risk created solely because of LEOs.

Should law enforcement allow us to run roughshod, the rewards for the risk would thereby be reduced by over 90 percent. So if you must be a dope salesperson, thank your friendly neighborhood officer for bolstering the value of that pocketful of nothing you're trying to slough off. Not sayin,' just sayin.'

And make no mistake, the rest of us need to seriously reshuffle and reassess the manner in which we regard law enforcement in general. They are primarily in place to protect our personal property as if it were their own. Placing their own asses at risk every single day over what? Because somebody reported someone stole their fcuking bike? And for a mere hundred bucks worth of junk, do we expect some cop to get their ass in gear and track down that piece of shit riding his new bicycle around? We would all be instantly overrun by instability if not for law enforcement. Accordingly, allow me to formally request that y'all kindly excuse my description to follow of certain individual agents regarding this entire drug war thing, OK? For one thing, such descriptions fly in the face of my previously misguided mindset. It needed to fly squarely in that face as I ignored the fact that laws were being broken. My feelings didn't make a shit back then, for I genuinely believed weed infractions should not be considered felonious, that these law enforcement guys were overreacting. What's their problem? News flash! My stupid ass was the one with the problem, OK? Major Tom to ground control. Come in. I sloughed it off as a mere dose of fun. A schedule A narcotic couldn't actually have that much of an adverse effect upon those perhaps scoring their head stash due to my actions, could it?

While I experienced several quite peculiar run-ins with several individual law enforcement people, as it were, it wasn't them out there overtly and indiscriminately breaking laws. The laws were and shall remain, knowingly and with free will, broken by none other than my big goofy ass. Shit. I'm still cool, still a renegade, and still not willing to accept any kind of "hug the world" bullshit mentality simply because, why, it feels good and it helps me connect with the younger people? Or check in to what is hip? Screw that. My message at this juncture to law enforcement in general? After careful assessment?

Please accept my sincere apology. For the unnecessary risks I created. For placing you in harm's way and for causing much angst down the line that I'm not even remotely aware of. You put an end to this callous attitude. Threw my ass in SCDC for over a decade, and they were successful in snapping me the fuck out of it. I needed snapping.

I own it. Wasting your time and my fellow citizens' money. No wonder there's no plaque hanging anywhere on my behalf. FM. As for those of you still reading, I shall preach to you regarding law enforcement under the exact premise I Dr. Phil'd up on your asses earlier in regard to weed itself and, what's worse, the culture of weed whereby "if it feels good, do it." That's such BS. Why don't we do it in the road? Yeah? More BS. Get a grip. Respect the one entity left in this crazy, messed-up world, allowing you the luxury of the precious few unalienable rights we have managed to cling to. Law enforcement wears it. Earns it. Every single day. It turns out, "we do need all those stinking badges." Badges allow you the pursuit of happiness, mind you, not the guarantee of happiness. The pursuit of it. Should you derive nothing therein, adopt the new necessity that we all owe law enforcement even more gratitude and respect, which they earn on a continuing basis, by the way. And for the record, this little spiel is not suck-up city, OK? I don't do suck-up, not now, not then, not ever. Don't need to. I do, however, acknowledge grit. Appreciating an officer as a simple thanks goes a long way. "Hey, thanks for getting my bike back." The gesture from you confirms your acknowledgment of the truth. An acknowledgment from you of your gratitude, for they deal with the crazed morons in society that you and I fake ass like we *cear* about (that's "care" pronounced in penitentiary mode, rhyming with "fear"). As flappin' if. And as a footnote? We don't have to repay them in full. Can't afford their actual worth to begin with. But we sure could through achievement one day make it possible through law enforcement. You remember this. Not saying, just saying.

Second up, cops don't make laws, you know? This is why we don't call 'em "lawmakers." We call 'em "law enforcement officers." When you develop an attitude over some "stupid-ass cop" getting in your way, remember that the way to avoid interaction with cops is not to behave or act in a manner contrary to laws they are sworn to enforce. That simple. They would much prefer zero interaction with you. No question. Should you disagree with any law as it stands, try lobbying to have the law changed. No use holding it against LEOs. Here's a news flash: get your flappin' driver's license, purchase adequate insurance, don't ride around Sally with weed smoke billowing out of your windows—*hello*—and stay the fcuk out of their way. They have plenty of attention to dole out your way should you flip stupid. You will lose. They will win. It's not a contest with any of 'em. All they want to do is go home tonight. And should you present yourself as an obstacle to this end? You're setting yourself up for a not-so-fun day. Easy enough.

Chapter 15
Not in My DNA

There was a lull between that first off-load and the next. I didn't hear from Flash for a while. I thought it would be a regular thing. Not so. Waiting and waiting. No updates. No flowers. One day, this other guy approached me about an off-load site. He said he wanted a backup plan up north of Hilton Head 'cause things were "getting hectic" down there. He had already flown over our place and was familiar with it through the multiple other groups' usage of it (mostly unknown to me), and he himself likely would have used it without our knowledge or consent but for the ole newly installed gate. Yea.

I told this fellow up front that I had a deal with a smuggler already, and he asked, "Who? Flash?" I was sorta taken aback the guy that even knew Flash. Most everyone and everything in the smuggling game were known to all the higher-ups. They didn't seem to mind everybody knew their business, for I suppose it gave the appearance of some omnipresent force to be reckoned with. Or as they tag this type of hype in the big house: "You be frontin,' you don't run nu'in."

The guy was adamant about seeing our place, and my guess is he wanted to make sure I held the key and that it was really family-owned property as I heard several reports of guys with no connection to the spot putting it out there on the open market for sale. We went on down to the spot and gazed around. Lo and behold, there were thousands of weed seeds everywhere. It was easy to discern if a boat or two or three had recently been off-loaded there. We knew nothing of it. Never did. The gate meant nothing. Turns out this fellow was all for show. He was a plant (not the Robert one) as well, sent to approach me (my guess at least, anyway) to determine if I was willing to allow some other group to use it possibly. Could it be that this guy went so far as to spread seeds everywhere to see if I'd own up to foreign activity. He could've been another of many trying to sell the place to other smugglers so somebody else could claim exclusivity to the place as the superb off-load site it was…and still is, for that matter. Maybe—God forbid—he was undercover. We didn't really know. Didn't much cear. Lemme quote my man Flash: "It ain't for everybody." I get exactly what he means by this proclamation. Ride this wave until it breaks up on the beach.

Drug smuggling, or the culture of weed and greed, and those of us all in and of that need come in to cash in on the hype. If you're able to post up and can exude an "I run something" persona, well, then you got a shot at it. Upon review of my evaluation of that choice and ability, I must now instead find solace in clinging to some positives. It was a positive to learn firsthand the basic nature of people, to come face-to-face with those so perceived that could be reliable, only to discover their dick-grabbing hand on a Bible pointing at me one day in open court. An image which shall always remain a permanent one.

The average *schmuck* is merely that. An average *schmuck*. Most herds in which we run are comprised of average *schmucks*. Don't look around now unless there's a mirror nearby. You're more likely than not running flesh deep in a few herds right now as the shoe likely fits just fine. Only you know this answer. The choices made by the average *schmucks* are usually based on convenience, money, or fear. If someone else is displaced by certain choices dialed in by another, tough shit. The majority of us can't think past this weekend, much less think why it is we ought to elevate our guts and grit beyond those of the rest of the world's buckets of shit. We have to take that step not to be a run-of-the-mill dweeb. I'm no average *schmuck*. I'm a cut-above *schmuck*. My choices didn't involve strapping on wires and trying to trade my prison time for someone else's. There's a time to, and this is anytime a crime is committed, and incidentally, most of the world defines crime as being an act that has a victim. Barring that, I can tell you *firsthand* that the reason not to flip is but one. Value of self. An older kingpin I more recently met and paid tribute to earlier said he never considered rat mode, never even remotely considered snitch-boy status, because of a statement perfectly describing the sentiments of all such men and women:

"It simply isn't in my DNA." More or Les says it all.

It isn't in my DNA either. I'm not protecting anybody. My body. My choice. My time. FokQ. His statement hit me hard. It aptly describes me too. My buddies. The ones in my trial. A big deal to us, though not to anyone else. Every snitch boy I know regrets the road so chosen.

Chickenshit Boulevard. Selling his soul to some agent and becoming his bitch. Listen, I regret taking an easy road back then knowing it'd likely lead to prison and cause major anxiety upon my mother. And it did. If there were a way, I'd change the entire drug game's participation; however, I wouldn't change one breath of my response to it.

Now, this DNA is totally resented and smacks the very face of every lower-level drug agent amid their primary objective in the drug game, in my opinion. To create snitch boys. Bitches. A game they cherish. A power they crave. It's a game they pursue under the guise of the law. Wherein they themselves transition these laws as granting them exclusive personal power over druggie types indifferent to the "dignity of the state." Here's a uDam Skippy flip for ya. We'll flip it around to indignity. And toss in a heartfelt FokQ to boot. And a little something for the state too. Ditto on the FU. And your fake-ass dignity. You pricks. After their own survival, of course, the main gig for agents is to create punks. Rats. Snitches. Flips. Call 'em whatever. All the same. You flip, you steal, you lie, you cheat, and you grope. All the same. You welch a bet. All the same. When the few of us with this special DNA decline to support their objective, demanding we adulterate that DNA to mimic theirs, they get pissed. You can't go back once you break weak. Once you turn bitch, you're forever bitch. Years later you'll end up embarrassed over it. Ashamed you were so much the moment's punk. You decline to discuss it. Ever. However, when you resist, their pursuits become a deeply personal pursuit. They try to entrap you; they threaten to arrest family members; they send hookers around, offering up free ass if "only you might score us an eight ball" so we may party. It didn't work, by the way. Skippy doesn't settle for the company of hookers. Not now, not then, not ever. SLED agents of the law sent hookers to see me, the luckless pedestrian, a couple times. Well, a couple times that I know of, offering up a few hundred bucks, hoping to score some cocaine since they could never attribute any drugs to my personal possession. Never did. Still haven't. Guess what? I knew it was a setup. Kept the three hundy and showed that skank-ass whore the door. Thanks for the donation, assholes. The hooker came back and confessed the next night. Still didn't want her rank; stink whore ass then either. I'm sure her parents are superbly proud of her lifestyle. Turns out she was arrested for prostitution but then decided to strap on wires and work undercover (in a different way). So much for the DNA running through her veins. How pitiful, a useless skank. Cue up Proverbs 11:22 (oh, get over it).

You know anyone who cheats on their spouse? You know anyone who has this edge to them that in your mind exposes their judgment as perhaps a bit on the conniving side? Well then, we can safely say you know someone who would rat your stupid ass instantly, at the drop of a dime. And whenever you spot that dime on the ground? On the floor? Don't pick it up! Don't bend over for ten cents! Someone dropped that dime, and whoever picks it up is more prone to being ratted. And the dimes drop like bricks. Faster and with more flair than any hat ever did. Law enforcement wanted my stupid ass to flip too. To rat the world. To come clean...all that horseshit. I had long ago decided not to cooperate and did in fact make this decision at about twelve years old. It's a mindset of resistance in many people's eyes as I'm approached about this subject frequently. Listen, people, it has nothing to do with resistance. And I totally get it, and I didn't then and don't expect anything in return. Didn't see it as posting up as some sort of tough guy and never once held back, being scared of repercussions for giving some clown up to law enforcement. Lots of times people ask, Why did you spare so-and-so? Why did you take the fall for so-and-so? Because it wasn't their fall; it was mine. That simple. And thank God for it. However, times do change, and in accordance with the wishes of said state handlers, the decision has finally been made to grant them their wish to lapse into their default mode. Which of course is the more easily managed rat-bitch mode. Fcuk them, there's nothing interesting or the least bit intriguing for snitches to write about. Therefore, to flip on that which needs flippin,' not merely to what they would deem fitting, to have ratted means to me now what it meant to me then. Dick. Means dick. Nothing. Therefore, let's reveal and let's flip the manner in which the state in all it's renown indignity regard us, resent us, wish to control us, and seek avenues to enter our world and seize our shit. Though, let's be careful regarding the mis-guided assumptions. As they usually emanate from building blocks of failure itself. As a get-back whereby Square D type nonproducers may sidestep their own inadequacies by coming after culprits like us. However, there's a tool in my arsenal -and in yours- that's served us well for an extended period of time. And good for you, too. It's called instinct.

Weed laws have and continue to illustrate this statement to the extreme. Federal weed laws have been in effect for decades, and sometimes those in authority choose to invoke such laws if it benefits them—or one of them—in some manner or manipulated strategy. But many times—as an obvious example—it is states where weed is legal now, the Feds choose to ignore completely their federal statutes as written criminalizing the possession of weed. This fact quells the argument from those by-the-book types who are hollering, "You broke the law, therefore you must pay the consequences." All laws may be rendered likewise discretionary because every decision to pursue a would-be defendant—from murder to jaywalking—must first meet the muster of a single law enforcement person in charge. And if there's nothing in it for the agent, there is no victim to answer to, or the victim is perceived as not worthy of the concern or effort? Many broken laws are knowingly ignored, traded out, or downplayed for some advantage by somebody in power. Drug enforcement was rendered much easier not because drug acts became more and more prevalent but because the laws themselves assumed an elevated level of punishment, of threat so harsh defendants were generally more inclined to rat; therefore, trading in rights and those threats of prison time for assets, information, or whatever a agent may desire at that particular crossroad. This is the motivation. Pure and simple. Every aspect involving the weed culture up until quite recently has been deemed illegal.

But hang on a sec. As stated, federal statutes proclaim it's illegal to possess weed, yet the Feds elect not to pursue millions of users in the several states that have determined possession thereof under certain parameters to be no longer illegal. And why do you suppose the several states decided to decriminalize lesser amounts of weed? Simple. They (bureaucrats) sought financial opportunity for them to reap the profits thereof, instead of the everyday slingers and growers of the once "dreaded" contraband. Of course, this approach requires the Feds to invoke their absolute discretion not to pursue these millions of weed possessors. Sure. They readily agreed not to. So much for that federal law.

There's important info for you to take from this right now. Every crime and every criminal pursuit depends on whether the person in authority wants to come after you or not. As a lesser example, ever had an occasion in which a patrol car blew by you and you just knew he was gonna turn around and collar you for speeding? But he never did. It's his sole discretion to pull you over or not. Maybe it was raining; maybe he was at the end of his shift. Maybe had his radar on standby mode. Whatever. The speeding part is irrelevant. It's his discretion that matters, for once you allow his access by your driving a bit fast, it's their call to make. Should he elect to pull you over, a lot of times the officer then factors into consideration your attitude. Should you treat this officer with the respect he deserves in the first place and expects in the second, chances are this encounter will have a better ending. They don't generally view us as speedsters anyway. But rather as a source of revenue. End of story. A very recent addition to bolster the revenue source is the ability of arresting officers to merely hit a button and print the citation. No more writing it. That took way too much time. Writing the ticket was viewed as tedious; they were more likely to let you go to save time. No more. You're sized. Profiled. Vehicle type. Age. Record. All in an instant. *Bam*. Here's your ticket, dickweed. Three minutes later we're back to running eighty. Couldn't outrun him. It was daylight. Come nighttime? Back in my wallowing-in-stupid days? I'm clocked at night from the opposite direction, and blue lights kick on. Simply fan the brakes a couple times, kick it up to about a buck-twenty, and that's a wrap. Outta sight equals chase over, baby. As in *o-v-a*. Listen to me now. Don't do that stupid shit. The roads are four times more crowded today. Not to mention police interceptors are fast as shit, and today's officers know how to drive and can play that little game better than you. Ain't happening.

Somewhere this very day, some fat ass drug agent is wiring up a scared-ass little mullet, in over his head, being threatened with decades in prison. Once you allow this step to be taken against you, accept the fact that you become this agent's bitch and you just got bent over. All he wants is your surrender, your fear, and your money. Law enforcement portrays all lawbreakers as dangerous, and for the most part, they are. However, law enforcement may also view some criminals more as an opportunity than of threat, but they dare not differentiate between the two so far as the stupid-shit public is concerned. We are Joe Public, don't you know, and Joe Public does not give two shits as long as the unwanted and many times unwarranted attention is directed toward some other slug. Someone else.

Here's a scene during the course of my first federal trial, where the "good cop" enters a room with four of us sitting there; likely we were sorta geeked up at the time. And he says something to the effect of, "Listen, boys, there's authorization to offer one of you guys a deal. As you are aware, we already have accumulated over one hundred fatty ratties' statements and testimonies should we need them. This deal offered would be one we call blanket immunity. Somebody among you may give us a statement that we've already *got* on record most likely over a dozen times anyway. The government is simply trying to lessen the cost of going to trial, as it's more cost-effective to try one less defendant. I'll be back in a few minutes, and you boys kick it around and decide who gets the get-out-of-jail-free card. So get your story straight."

Well, there we all sat, no one saying much, but who wouldn't like to not go to jail? Me, not intending to bullshit you either, and I will confess for a brief reshuffle. My thinking was, well, if my guys determine I'm the logical recipient, what the hell. And *yes*, despite the DNA, Skippy had a brief hesitation to cave. Shit, I ain't no Superman. Just some slug trying to make it to the next day.

All of a sudden, my man Charles Devenraux Moauxdelawn stands up and proclaims, "OK, fellas, as the man said, let's get our story straight. And here is that story made easy so we can all be on the same page. Check it now;"

"There ain't no fucking story. We say nothing; we have nothing for them. Nothing. Dick. Any questions? I didn't think so. We grew up with class. We aren't anything like the other cracker pieces of shit in this trial. Years from now none of this will matter." And with that, my guy takes a seat.

And the three of us go into total wolf mode. "Yeah, take that, biatch, my man! Shiiiiit, that's just what I wanted to say and was waiting on one of y'all." It's like my guy reached over and smacked the dog shit out of me. Exactly what was needed in the heat of that very pivotal decision. Another shining example of how one's life is so influenced by our choices of association. Holy hand glider, Batman brings us all back to Earth. Wouldn't trade this guy for the world. May you have such a friend. Kept us in our lanes. The true safeguard against a flippin' punk.

Chapter 16
The Four Knots to Blossom

When you settle for a whore, don't squawk when you end up with one or as one. Here's a little bonus for all you seekers of contentment. For you sons and daughters electing to avoid that easy ride down Degenerate Boulevard, bouncing around from degenerate to degenerate and believing the next one somehow an improvement over the latest slug, you have merely revealed your own lack of discretion. How many times we gotta kick that can down the road only to discover one day that the road does not go on forever? That the road has a dead end as you sit there amid a bunch of dented-up cans with that 'feed me a mega-shit-sandwich' look on your face? A big, fat dummy. Try invoking the Four Knots Rule like I learned to do when it comes to one's wife, husband, or significant other. Each of these knots represents a decade of toil and torment, trying to discover the real. And mind you, as I advised my own kid to consider, in so doing you are more likely to end up with a gratifying, loving, and appreciative partner once the other side realizes. May I present to you, with pleasure, the four knots:

Knot a stupid ass.

Knot a broke ass.

Knot a drunk ass.

Knot a slut ass (for a guy's reference) or knot a perv ass (for a gal's).

Bam. There's some happiness for you. These are what's referred to as lifelines dangling from the sky, defining and identifying all of our very nature. Sorta like vines from all types of trees in this infinite jungle, we can grab hold of 'em and maneuver our flight path through the dense terrain of countless, endless faces. These lifelines are sometimes easier to define and to hold on to when there's a knot at the end of them as we go swinging through the jungle. Take that "knot a stupid ass" lifeline as an example. Everybody senses these lifelines just dangling there, you know, as we go swinging along, seeking an easier pathway. You meet a person, and that lifeline of a stupid ass is without that critical knot identifier? That's your sign to let go of that MF and try and grab another one possessing said knot, thereby making it so much easier to hold on to the real. You gonna grab some stupid-ass vines, and if it doesn't offer you up a big, fat, proud knot, you gotta hang on loosely until you grab one with that knot. No knot happening means it's big time easier to let go of. Let it go, man; turn it loose and simply walk your happy ass away.

And allow me to express to you some basics I learned the hard way about relationships. All sorts of relationships. There's business and working, there's neighbors and just passing-through relationships. The one, as we all know, with the most profound impact on our lives is the romantic one. The husband-and-wife one. The boyfriend-and-girlfriend one. Once we figure that one out—that significant other one—the rest of 'em tend to seem a touch easier. That main one shouldn't be a chore, you know? It should be a fifty-fifty deal. Ideally it should be one in which both parties want the association and attention of the other. In contrast to one in which one of the partners needs the other. That won't work unless both wish to fake ass the gig itself. It should promote culture and commonality and thrive amid mutual respect as a given, in a situation where we really do care. I'm a pro at it now; 'course it took fifty-five years or so, but it finally came to me. At least consider you're saving a little time in this arena (ruh-roh, my best gal just pulled up, so I gotta put this on hold until later).

OK, she bolted. Don't like to write when she's around. Why? 'Cause this would be our time. As we uncork a bottle of red time. The enjoyment of companionship time. The celebrating that we aren't anywhere close to that lonely time. Our contentment is in each other's company time. Celebrating the drink that we're drinking is not the one BJ referred to as "loneliness." A wonderful thing. Spin it around for the subtle piece of nuance is. We always make a toast with our first glass of red. Be happy you have someone in your life giving a shit enough about you to bitch to you about taking the trash out in the first place. Another toast comes to mind: "It just hit me; here's to you babe; sharing exactly the same qualities as my preferred wines...leggy and rich."

OK? My gal was not the least bit offended and understood we were simply enjoying life amid a bit of good time banter. She knows a little tongue-in-cheek is mostly for humor's sake. For we know the road doesn't go on forever. Life is good, people. Be sure to wake up and live it. The times to be serious should 'bout equal the times to have a little fun. Don't you think? Keepin' it light. Cheers.

Wherein we are hereby delivered to a few words about jealousy. To me jealousy is the number-one indicator of stupidity. Why on Earth would you seek someone's company specifically or exclusively when that someone has made it clear that they would rather be someplace else or in someone else's company? WTF? Can someone please explain this to me? Are you fcuking stupid? Are you? Why do people call their exes when they first break up thirty times a day? Or more? Texting nonstop? If that someone would rather be someplace else, why the fcuk would you insist upon their continuing the headliner's slot with you when they've made it clear that's a wrap? You gotta be stupid. Are you just plain stupid? That's the main knot both of you just gotta learn to seek it out. Are you perved up or cuckoo for Cocoa Puffs off the chart for somebody whose wishing you'd free, free, set them free? It's a matter of one's right to associate. To freely associate. And without the obstacle of your silly ass demanding the kid gloves and demanding their time to at least let you down easy? If they change their mind and announce directly or through actions there're no longer down with your plan, so be it. Ride out. Find another. Free, free, set them free. What are you? Desperate? We refer to this condition as "being mesmoed up." Give it a rest, would ya? Cry out loud if you must. Partners weren't placed on this earth to entertain our stupid asses or your stupid ass. Your daddy didn't tell you this? Well, he should have. Would you want your daughter or son to be smacked by some undisciplined asshole gathering jollies going around hitting people? Then apologize the next day? "Oh, they just have trouble sometimes expressing their feelings." Horseshit. Gimme a break. What pricks.

Now something just for the ladies. It's so much easier to break it down for you girls. 'Course I can only break it down from the standpoint of being the guy as relates to experiences over the decades. Just opinion based on what has revealed itself to me many, many times. It seems to boil down to this one thing. A bit crude, perhaps, but some good advice that will spare you a bunch of wasted time and memories you'll wish to have avoided. Check it now...

And check it out really good. *Are* you ready?

The less you sling that ass, the better off you'll be.

Did you get that? The less you sling that ass, the better off you are. It's true. I've seen it time and time again. Oh, it may be more fun. Oh, you might be more popular. But file this away for safekeeping. No man wants a whore for a wife. No kid has ever wished for his mom to be slutty. Not even Jesus, and He is very forgiving. Even making reference to it in His book, in Proverbs 11:22, to be exact: "As a jewel in a pig's snout, so is a fair woman without discretion." Not to preach to you, but it's a dead end. And in the end, it will simply be you and your tired, cheapened, and worthless ass. That nobody wants. That you can't flappin' give away on Seventh Avenue. Burned up and burned out and tossed away. And it ain't better to burn out either. Well, maybe in death. But certainly not in ass. It's far better to simply fade away.

Footnote here. It's certainly not my place to delve into people's sexuality. We can agree on this one, no doubt. It's your business. Exactly how it ought to be. The term "slingin'" ass more so refers to the number of, not the frequency with. There. The fewer chapters in that numbers-count book, the better. Just my opinion. I am not good at this topic to begin with. And from a personal standpoint, if I can't be with the one I love, there is no lovin' for the one I'm with. As couples age together, it becomes more and more beneficial to share the concepts of togetherness. Part of how we are designed. It's something we all need, not to mention the contentment it ideally delivers. And let's not forget that there are numbers at play here too, even with intimacy. Aside from the spark. Sure. Let's break it down just for the halibut.

Scuse me while I whip this out. Relax, everybody. Just a calculator, people. Let's see...525,000 minutes in a year. All righty then. Intimacy, say...comes in at around twenty, thirty times a year average (counting youth and aging—averages). Maybe? OK. So we dream a little. Whaaaaat. Two or three hundred minutes per year? Max? Yeah, right. You know how much time we actually spend in boink-up mode in Blissville? Try 0.0004 to 0.0007 percent of one percent of the total time in a year. What's the point? That intimacy doesn't require very much time out of life. However, it is part of an equation of balance. Of living. Do this. Simply discover your mate and live with that person. Love that person. And hey, now, bank this. You can't make anybody love you either. You can't fake ass any "spark." It's there, or it ain't. Bonnie Raitt sings about it, and it's easy to sing along. But man, oh man, once we identify that spark as real, then we discover that love and share the glory of culture, music, wine, and good company. You will then know peace and proceed to all the everyday wonderful things this world truly has to offer. You're not drinking that drink they call loneliness. And ain't it grand? All righty then, enough blush. Not to get too far into all this, let's get back to the business of slinging some dope instead, but first...

Another uDam Skippy story. A right clever one at that. It was a gift to me from my dear ole dad. It was his attempt to prevent me from ever becoming some clown all stupid up about girls, and I gotta tell ya, it worked.

It was fourth grade at recess one day, and this boy out of the blue lamented, "Guess what, Skippy? You got born because your mommy and daddy screwed."

Well, that was quite the traumatic statement to me just playing on the monkey bars at recess across the street from Hampton Elementary School in good ole Walterboro, South Carolina. So once I was home, the inquiry was directed to my dear ole dad. A good ole guy named Keeby. He had to grab a beer and clear the throat a few times, "Oh boy."

Then proceeds into this long soliloquy about where babies come from (given that he was talking only to the wall). Gestation. Birth. Breast feeding. All quite boring, don't cha know?

Then he said, "Any questions?" Now wait just a minute here, you ain't gettin' off that easy, my man.

"Yeah, what about this screwing thing?"

He simply told me, "Pretty much true, kid."

OK, how does that work? And here's where he took the low road and told me screwing is a big deal, even though it is somewhat overrated.

"What do you mean, Pops?"

"Well, it's known as the 'blossom.' It's where very young girls don't actually develop the physical ability to do these things until just before they become old enough to get married and maybe have a family. Usually this process begins at around nineteen to twenty-one years old. And this being the case, it's understood they lack the ability until they sprout the blossom far later in life, as they mature. So there's no use wasting a bunch of time on this and that when this or that is not even quite possible just yet. Do you get it? So while you boys wait for these blossoms to happen, we dads of the world simply encourage our young sons to pursue other things. Just as we were shown to do in our youth. Play sports, join the Boy Scouts, mow yards, and have paper routes. You know all the things you're beginning to do to occupy your time. You water-ski and fish…things like that."

Hey. Made sense to me. And was viewed as a total explanation, after which my ass simply went outside and played roll-a-bat with neighbors Richard and Man. Armed with the explanation and my inside scoop on the new truth, no doubt. And during my entire upbringing from then on, people would unwittingly confirm this theory as truth itself. Just as it was processed in my little world, albeit thoroughly unknown to anyone else. Sorta sloughed it all off as fact and went about the business of growing up.

Then flash-forward, me and a buddy were out water-skiing on the Waccamaw River in Conway, South Carolina, in dear ole dad's boat with three girls from our church. We are all around fifteen, sixteen. And my buddy, Ricky Gore, a totally hip little kid, says, "You know, Skippy, that girl with us? Connie? Word has it, she likes to throw down, you know what I'm saying?"

"Well, sure, Ricky, but how's that even possible? She's only sixteen and not exactly into the ole blossom thing yet, right? We can make believe and all, but it's still fun out on the river skiing with 'em. They're our girls, you know? I like it how they laugh and stuff. And bring sweet tea and fried chicken."

"Yeah, you probably right. Hey, Skippy, what's the blossom mode thing, anyway?"

Poor Ricky. He didn't have an active daddy in his life. Later on, word was that he ended up getting a girl pregnant, and they were only seventeen. Not the case in the world of Skippy. Thanks to dear ole Keeby and his allowing my learning which paths to living a little wiser.

And so it went on like this for my ass for several years. Oh, those times we were missing. And as high school began to reveal itself to me a bit further in, it very gradually began to sink in—that just maybe I'd been slightly misinformed. Ya think? One day a room mate of mine went so far to ask me, "This blossom thing, is this when you're thinking to give a girl flowers?"

One episode comes to mind. A very pretty girl named Karen from Beaufort. Loved her. Had that spark in her company. All the components. She late teens. Kinda implied things. Like staying over for the night. The little hints. However, my ass was so concerned regarding her blossom status and all; she assumed I wasn't interested and eventually simply drifted away from our quaint little scene. Never told her. Too embarrassed. uDam Keeby.

Then one fateful day—or slightly more descriptive, one night, as it were—in a slightly inebriated state in my early twenties, well, a rather, shall we say, spunky college woman blossomed my ass up firsthand. And that was that. Hello. And years later? there was a new sitcom on TV called *Blossom*. About a young gal trying to figure life out? I'd sorta look around with the slightest of doubt and raise an eyebrow and wonder, was ole dad hittin' on something here? Now that there is a TV show called *Blossom*? All of that made up too? Zero basis for the theme here? Back to the age of innocence, missing those simpler times, just thumbing through the memories. Nah. 'Course not. Just a clever name for a sitcom, I reckon. Thanks Pops.

Here's a uDam question for ya. Anybody. How come I hear this all the time where people constantly telling girls, "You go girl."

"You go girl."

Where exactly do all the people barking this statement out all day at girls, suggesting the subject girl go to?

Some random 'go-to' space somewhere? A random time? And how come girls I know a bit more with their shit together seem not nearly as likely to hear the term 'you go girl' chant barked out at them?

Just trying to ponder a little here, that's all.

And while we're at it, we hire dozens of girls and grown ladies at our several businesses over the years and I notice many of 'em, especially the younger ones, go around saying, "I'm sorry."

"I'm sorry." All day long. Over mostly meaningless nonsense, as if renders the instant time as hyperspaced some where else. Why all the 'I'm sorrys?' They didn't do anything to be sorry for. Most of the time I hear it is when they discover themselves in the same vicinity as me or as another shopper in a store or something.

Seems when we allow our daughters to walk around constantly proclaiming they're sorry, well, I believe this is not healthy for the girls to spew out every six minutes. For one day, the I'm sorry brigade might actually wake up to some notion that they actually are sorry, and this being the new norm, respond to everyday societal interaction as a lesser valued participant. I don't know why to toss this in here, but dammit man I hear it all the time and to me it seems to foster some subservient value in the poor girl's head. Maybe I should stick to tales of weed instead. I'm sorry.

Chapter 17
Numbers, Baby: 12K Flight

Quickly, people. Here's a quick test for ya. How many thousands are in a million? If there is more than a millisecond's hesitation on your part for the right answer, then you are not what we refer to as a numbers person. Not being a numbers person renders us more susceptible to the hustle of this life.

I really enjoy numbers. The mindset of numbers. They don't lie. And they don't flip either. They remain true to both God and nature, which you can't say about much else in this world. Numbers reveal to us practically all relevance there is to know. Numbers merely exist. With zero feelings. Gotta love that. They don't care about how you feel. They do not care if you understand them, believe they are too complicated or easy, or consider them boring or exciting to begin with. They simply offer empowerment and, in rather subtle manner, a degree of relaxation as the default go-to gut check of facts. Ask that ole flattop as he comes groovin' up slowly: one and one and one is three. *Truth.* That's the basis for numbers. It's why, in my opinion, today's education system shies away from teaching math. Purposeful ignorance. Why? Once a person is indoctrinated by the absolute truth of numbers, they are rendered more familiar with truth in absolute terms. This enables numbers people to possess the skill to recognize when they are confronted with nontruths.

The ability to think for one's self in the arena of numbers endows us all with wisdom whereby we fill voting booths as a more sure-footed and therefore informed citizenry.

I strive to think in terms of mathematics as numbers precludes our drifting away with feel-good imaginations intending to offer distractions, surely colliding with the foundation of truth we cherish through the honesty of numbers in most every single other category of life. Most successful people are good at numbers. Most dumb asses are void of the advantage of numbers. Which one are you? Still, numbers don't give a shit. It's our choice to discover them or not. Ever dream of numbers? How strange it was to relate said dream to my best gal, who lamented that it wouldn't strike her that I was the number four. "It's the wrong shape." OK, what's my number, then? The number zero. Do tell, please. Well, it turns out that zero more accurately depicts the shape of an asshole than any other number. Why I oughta… hey, if you can't enjoy a humorous spice-up with your best gal, perhaps you'll deserve your best gal a bit less. Quite funny.

My first numbers lesson occurred once upon a time when a major league druggie-type smuggler contacted me regarding a run he requested be considered for a special delivery. Telegram for Mongo. It involved the use of a small airplane, to which my response was, "My guy's not into hauling dope, at least not yet, but I'm working on him."

He responded, "Oh, Skippy, this is not about hauling any dope. Just need you to fly to Richmond and pick up a little child's portion of cash. Pure cash. Think you could pull this one off? Don't much like the idea of that much cash being exposed on the interstate system, in an automobile, where the likelihood of some sort of intervention ordeal is much greater. The trip pays twelve thou for you boys to deliver back this sorted minor little dustup. What say you?"

I said consider this a go, that we'd be in touch with him after speaking with the real pilot and scheduling accordingly, at which time the instructor guy contacted me, and he said, "Sure, since we're only grabbing a little bit of cash, let's go."

As was common practice in the world of aviation back then, the smaller the plane, the less attention it attracted in terms of possibly being of a nefarious nature. So off we go, departing the infamous Frogmore International Airport and heading north. Fifteen minutes into the trip, the instructor guy hits me with the question: "So OK...How much money are we picking up anyway?"

"Boss man said it was around three mil."

He fired back, "Do you think you're going to get three million bucks in that little briefcase you're sporting, or is there something else in it that's questionable?"

"Well, no. The briefcase is empty. Thinking to place the money in it. Why else do I have it with me?"

He continued to grill me on this, asking what denominations we might expect the bills to be in, and I gave him these vague answers like, "How the hell am I supposed to know?" Well, seemed not the right response.

Enter the numbers game. 867-5309. Not those kinda numbers, calling an imaginary lover. But the real numbers. Let's think. Imagine you're in a Cessna 172 and just made a 360-degree turn. Just kidding. You'd be going in the same direction. Of course. The only time I witnessed the instructor guy slip. The control tower told him to turn around while taxiing at Savannah International, and he said OK, I'll give it the ole 360. He meant a 180. Anyway, just to remind him to never forget that slipup. But I do much appreciate his skill, and, oh yeah, that still-being-alive thing too. But anyway, back to the Cessna, banking a hard left toward home.

Hey…all we needed was the smallest plane (for the three mil). Didn't tell him the amount of cash we're picking up. Simply said let's go. Then the questioning began: How much is it again? A touch over three mil. What are the denominations again? Assuming it's street money mostly, twenties? How many twenties in a million? Quickly, children! Somebody? Anybody?

Everybody? One million divided by twenty. Fifty thousand bills. Right? How much does a dollar bill weigh? One gram. How much does a twenty-dollar bill weigh? One gram. How many grams are in a pound? Any druggie type oughta know that answer. So 50,000 grams divided by 454 grams per pound equals what? Why, that's 110 pounds. Times three, maybe a little over. Plus whatever it happens to be wrapped or packaged in. That equals 330 to 350 pounds or so.

We turned around and had to go grab a bigger free bird. The instructor guy was disgusted with such ignorance. As was right there revealed through my void of basics. That was the instant of epiphany for this dam Skippy. Non-numbers people are regarded as morons by people of numbers. Regarded as in the fcuking way also. You can change this. You need not be perceived as stupid. Or in the way. Apply the discipline from within. The luxury of focus. The rewards of grit. All of which are adulterated by the use of weed—just a pass-along to ya. Learn what's at stake. Learn what makes you more of a target for unscrupulous types wishing to displace you of your money based largely upon your ignorance of numbers. Discover why you play the lottery. You're a flappin' moron and can't calculate odds and truth. The lottery commission thrives on your stupidity and rakes off about 20 percent of lottery play for their so-called administrative (i.e., bookie) fees. Casinos all refer to this as their "rake." 'Course the dignity of our state elects not to openly discuss this rake…ahem, ahem, admin fee. They don't want us to know about the hundreds of millions they rake in over the years. Lack the ability to earn it through commerce, though it's perfectly OK to extract most of it from those dumb masses that can least afford the constant losses.

Look around when you go into a convenience store. Who do you see primarily purchasing lottery tickets? Think about it. It ain't no rocket scientists lining up thinking they are going to get that one-in-one-hundred-million shot today. It is typically larger people in beat-up cars where you have to slam the rusted-out doors in order to shut 'em, and three-to-one against they don't have any insurance. Not sayin,' just sayin.' Many people void of numbers are enslaved by the cult of stupidity. Are you in that cult? How much do you make a year? You know a lot of people will say they make twenty dollars an hour, or twenty-five dollars an hour, but they don't really know their annual salary. You need to know what you're dealing with when you deal with people, and a primary part of this equation is how much they make. Their motivation. How much is at stake? And how is their salary tied to yours? Let's start with you. Say you make thirty bucks an hour. The short answer is that you make $60,000 a year. This should be a default setting in your mind every time the subject pops up. If nothing more than for the sake of being on your toes and having an inkling of what drives the driven.

Tune in to the present portrait of here and now and what surrounds you. Motivations, et cetera. It's really simple to calculate anyone's primary number. Their salary. It's forty hours a week times fifty weeks (with a couple off for sickness vaca, what have ya.). It equals two thousand hours per year. Being paid twenty-five bucks an hour grosses you how much? Double the hourly wage (for twenty-five per hour, that would be fifty) and simply attach three zeros behind it, and bada bing, there's your answer. Fifty grand. You make fifteen bucks an hour? Thirty grand per year. You gotta know this stuff if nothing else but for the sake of knowing this stuff. For crying out loud, it ain't a Rubik's cube. It ain't Japanese algebra. It's confidence and some order over chaos. And what in the world does a math lesson have to do with the excitement and rigors of smuggling weed?

Easy. To embrace the numbers is to have the capacity to figure out the odds. Most normal Joes are able to discern this, and to their credit, they have. Then they decided to avoid such frivolous pursuits amid seriously questionable odds. Also notable, within the scope of numbers, many truths are revealed in more clearly understood terms.

Let's do a review of bigger-boy salaries in general. In sports especially. Alluding to that entertainment factor. For instance, when we hear about coaches, some coaches in college football are paid a salary of, say, twelve million bucks a year (some much, much more), we need to understand the significance of this money just so it's understood. That way we will be less of an idiot and more of a person getting it, getting where motivations come from, and relating more to what's exactly at stake. Getting to what actually drives this entertainment and all entertainment venues. To a mild degree, it's sportsmanship and the nurturing of young men and athletes in general. However, most of this industry is defined by the money, honey. As well, it's to some about not dwelling on the money part too much so you believe that maybe it is about the competition, personalities, and emotion. While numbers people are perfectly able to embrace the concept value of entertainment itself, we remain keenly aware that the mechanism fueling the engines is cash driven. Capitalism. And that twelve million annual salary of the coach? A festive six-thousand dollars per hour. Hey, don't go hatin' now, OK? If they were not worth the money they wouldn't command the chunk.

Nothing says you can't be a coach, you know. Sweat how much you make, not what another earns. Simple.

Chapter 18
Get Outta Jail Free

En route to discovering how weed was the flavor of the day and opened doors for enforcement people and opened doors to other worlds, wealth was a huge consideration. And this is the part where people seem a bit intrigued by the doors, opportunities, and intrigue it opened for me and others similarly situated. All brought on by or through the numbers and mountains of cash.

Take a ride with me down Ribault Road, if you will, in the quaint little town of Beaufort, South Carolina. You know, sometimes I don't know why, but this ole town just seems so hopeless. Oh, we miss ya, T. P. Nothing, but the dead of night back in my little town. Early to mid-eighties, it is. Lollygagging my way back from a weed stash house, holding a mere couple hundred pounds of some freshly smuggled weed in the trunk, waiting for pickup by an out-of-town driver. Done it many, many times. Couldn't risk them taking it's possession at the stash house, for if they were busted, 95 percent of them would have led the cops directly back to it.

Just breezin' along in the usual "shit up the depends" mode when all of a sudden, blue lights flash on as they whiz by me on patrol from the opposite direction. Hey, the decision to attempt to outrun LEOs is an instant one as we've already reviewed. As was mine that night. Step one: stomp that petal on the right. Step two: fan the petal on the left, giving the impression you are slowing down and seeking a place to pull over. Step three: once you lose sight of the pursuing blue light special, it's over, so let's kick it. I hung a quick right down Bay Street toward downtown and whipped it into our Batcave apartment, some twenty or thirty feet below street level. Hey, one more exciting kiss-off. All is good. Feel me?

Some two minutes later, a squad car eases down the driveway, crushing a few of those displaced rocks with that sound that'll never be forgotten, lights off. From the Crown Vic a police officer steps out, I knew proceeded to relay to me in a whisper that our place was under surveillance, and he inferred an early morning raid was likely. Sooner than later. "This one's on me, Skippy; next time, no get-out-of-jail-free card. Have a nice night."

The guy knew my story. We had a chunk of weed stashed there, and I was bringing it and slingin' it. Why didn't he collar me right there and then? Beats me. I proceeded to rid the premises of all contraband and get the hell out of town, transporting everything back to this trick little stash house twenty-six miles away in Yemassee, South Carolina. My thanks to this fellow years later—though you are deceased, I shall never give you up. Not then, not now, not ever. A DNA thing, don't you know?

You do the crime, you do the time. We've all heard it, right? Here's a truer statement we touched upon as to every crime: its prosecution is 100 percent discretionary. Check it out now: You heard it first on *W-I-N-O* Radio. That's right, I know that when it comes to any and *every* crime, the prosecution has 100 percent discretion as to whether to pursue it or not. Just as the process of identifying and elevating any act to a criminal one is 100 percent discretionary. According to fed and state statutes, I committed crimes against the dignity of the state through my affiliation with weed by either possessing it, consuming it, possessing it in higher amounts, transporting it from one jurisdiction to another, or even discussing it in any capacity with another person (defined as conspiracy). Every law ever written, from the Ten Commandments to today's endless procession of federal controls to homeowners association rules, is a matter of complete discretion, each and every one a matter of procedures and hoops set up based entirely upon any select whim of the day.

Whether to create law; whether or not its objectors are deemed in compliance or not; when or whether its enforcement is viable or not; and to what extent punishment is put in effect, whereby the law's integrity is rendered viable—all are based on the discretionary judgment. One person in authority is all it takes.

Speaking of smuggling weed, speaking of "better than a movie," why become involved with smuggling in the first place? It is called "Thank God for the shot at it." Why not? It was just weed. Didn't seem criminal to me; it didn't seem as if any victims were created. WTF. Gave me a purpose, whereas I lacked the proper info to identify any of the purposes spelled out so succinctly by older men and women, much less from, God forbid, within the confines of the one religion we dare not embrace either—our own. Instead...well, here's the rest of the story with a degree of entertainment value, but for nothing more than your attention amid the abundant collections of hype. And before we get going, and speaking of God, allow me to proclaim in no uncertain terms, right here, right now.

I'm a Jesus guy. OK? Pure and simple. I was always this way; frankly, it just took some time to kick it in. Jesus is just all right with me. I don't resent the fact that He chose us. Chose me. God seems to trump everything else. We proclaim we live on Edisto Beach, Charleston, or anywhere and say, "It's heaven." However, when we add emphasis in a text, we resort to "OMG." Right? We don't say "Oh my Edisto" or 'Oh my money." We all go with "Oh my God." So who is the boss in our world? Should you wish not to read antics by someone subservient to a higher power? Slam the son of a bitch shut and go worship the common degeneracy. Or worship your earth amid all its devine dirt. After all, all of us crave religion. Something we look up to for balance, for definition. Seems to boil down to whatever it may be that we choose to worship likely invokes some representative thereof as providing an accompanying 'god' demanding our allegiance. Is our Earth warming? Maybe so. Is this a serious gig in your book? So you feel should we elevate the earth to a so called god that this action renders the earth itself as worthy our worshipping of it? For it is a god? How 'bout money? Or power? Or dope, alcohol, sex, or food? My take on earth worship? If it's warming and becomes quite problematic? There will be a future very smart person able to remedy the ordeal. Remember, our people are truth. Are with intellect and will figure the remedy as we have in many other instances. Therefore, allow this tangible truth soak in a little. That we shall be provided a brilliant mind one day as to resolve any warming results of such our deplorable actions. Same with other false gods. They will be proven false insofar as their value to us. The only God having showed me the way thus far in this life… is Jesus. I tried many others. The wretched excess one too. Jesus remains my last guy standing in the world of uDam. Simple enough.

You are rendered less likely to seek a skewed truth when you possess truth in its default mode. That lack of real. Instead you may find yourself seeking out other sources, more likely needing the crutch of alcohol, drugs, or some other bullshit intellectual shitting up your scene with horseshit rhetoric. You are a hundred times more likely to fall for this crock of shit when void the voice of your creator. Ain't no wtf earth created you. God created you and granted you dominion and control of the earth; or at least your place on it. Now, mind you, I do care, just not all that much. This is simply an opinion, OK? What I can tell you is that education was delivered to me in the most gratifying terms. Forming a mindset of confidence and contentment. It's nice to have graduated, let me tell ya.

As for religion, just so we're clear, in the world of my former world, the entire Jesus thing was adverse to the run-and-gun herd I elected to run with. As I aged, and inadvertently matured, I discovered there was more inclination to dance with the one that brung me. Well, I believe Jesus brung me. I believe that I did not come from a fcuking monkey but that I'm a descendant of the non-sixth-day man, Adam, who was, according to Genesis, created after all the more famously sixth day created people. This proclamation made, and I fully recognize this position, turns some of you weed burners off. I make no attempt to antagonize, disrupt, or shock the consciousness. Suppose you would rather I stick with the fun shit. And leave religion out of it. Well, religion is why I believe we're all here. Why ignore it? I've got a boatload of religion that just recently made it to the off-load site. It's taking me a few decades to muscle it off so it could be accessed. It could be that one day I'm deemed part of another conspiracy defying in some manner the dignity of a warming earth. And some sheriff finds the chance to arrest me. I don't give a flying fcuk about anyone's thoughts on my take on religion, for it's my business. As I am without hesitation 100 percent, allowing for your own interpretations in the exact same capacity. It's a God-given right, and to those who don't believe there is a God, you are still entitled to this right. Right? In your world, I might assume you consider your particular rights to have fallen out of the sky. OK, fine. My wish for you is total happiness and peace. Let's have a beer.

I gotta throw some Skippy logic in here. Just a dash. I regard these truths to be self-evident. They're my truths and are not likely on the radar, much less absolute, in your world, just the current prevailing mindset in mine. Consider it an opinion, OK? My rebuttal, if you will, is more of a balance-up against our mainstream culture attempting to indoctrinate us to accept concepts of some sorta non-God utopia. Yo, man, I was sucked into it as well by yielding to my own preferences for easy and for longing for the peculiar acceptance of hip and cool, man. More so based upon image and perception than reason and the real. Running with the herd, baby, which I did, careful not to get too far out front, and thank goodness, I did eventually manage to veer off that path with a very grateful sigh of relief. Was easily reeled in miles straight up above the chore of deliberate indifferences, whereby temperance and character did finally overcome frivolity.

Stand fast, therefore, in the liberty where Jesus has made us free. Very powerful. For we wrestle not against flesh and blood but against the principalities, powers, and rulers of darkness in this world. Man, oh man. Good book, baby. Low-hanging fruit we're challenged every day to simply take a bite as it passes by. Come on…it can't be that bad. The nonstop double-dog dare-you to imagine. Hey, let's imagine there's no heaven and no religion too. See there? And why can't we just do it in the road? We're bombarded by very smart people suggesting that their way is the way to our seeking of the finality of truth itself. Whose truth is it to begin with? The new civility of more easily achieved behavior requires the far less discipline so invoked than does the power of our ultimate minesetting critical within our circle safeguarding our very survival itself.

Not once have I ever listened to these vast legions of drive-by intellectuals apply their keen and gifted sense of creativity or imagination to suggesting, well, what if? What if the options of godliness and discipline are viable? What if we need not draw the map but merely follow one already laid out before us? What do ya say we review that one? What if? Owning the mere chance to be on point? What if we forgo the proven successes of our religion and unveil an easier, more deliberate path to contentment? Well, my ass discovered such the path. This is all I'm attempting to convey here. A simple, small step for Skippy. One giant leap for truth amid folly. Is it alright with you that might I imagine there is such our God?

Yo, man, I possess imagination and am capable of processing and expressing creativity. I am blessed by faith, not at all challenged in defiance of it. I am perfectly capable of translating what it means to me. No need for some culted up or perved up pope or priest. No need for some rabbi hollering about how Jesus exists, He ain't quite made it here yet. Oh, really? Well, I happen to believe he has already. Label me total sap, should you choose. I don't give a shit. Run tell that one, asshole. Save that one, OK? I'm faith-based. Totally so as is my religion requires. It saved me and revealed the better me. Maybe not quite the intrigue of fast cars and stacks of Benjies, but lemme tell you how it fosters gratitude. How it transforms questions into answers and hope into contentment. Likewise the more prepared you become to ward off the unbelievable challenges continuing to assault us in every direction, the better shot you'll have to hold and share through understanding the attempted assaults upon us all. What is the purpose of it all? You'll at least possess an answer, a pathway, or a basis for hearing the starting gun to pursue that answer.

I only came to read our Bible in solitary confinement. Genesis. Eyes opening when locked down in solitary, minus any and all distraction. We all ask, "Where did I come from?" It states that man was created on day six. OK, fine, I thought. A few pages deeper, Adam is created in God's image. God blew the breath of life into Adam's nostrils. Got me asking, were the sixth-day people created in God's image? Did their nostrils receive His first breath of life? Does the symbolism translate to actual? What if it does? Could it be the breath of life thing represents the instant we were granted individualism? Intellect? Compassion? Character? Maybe. Maybe not. What if it's true? Or did we garner these virtues through our evolution from once upon a time being a fcuking monkey? Did we come from monkeys? Well, then, explain how they're still monkeys? What about the feel good of inclusion where 'no monkeys left behind'? You mean, you're at ease with the concept of our DNA having passed through some major changes where over time we went from a mere monkey scratching his ass and thumping his balls on a tree branch, to being able to launch F-16s off a floating city? Damn man. That's some strong shit we're puffing on.

It was just little ole me in a solitary cell with time to ponder. Meanwhile, back at Swank Island, I credit Christianity with my identity. I'm about embracing the attributes defining character, intellect, creativity, and even compassion. Once I peeled back all the superficial bullshit, I was left with an unequaled energy of gratitude that little ole no-freaking-body me has a history that just might be worthy of my ultimate regard. That I'm a son of Adam and Isaac, whose name shall always be upon us. Hey, you out there in the cold, can you hear me? If Adam is the very first man and we all descendants thereof, why are the pages and pages of who begat who tracing genealogy back to Adam? Why would this matter if all mankind came from Adam from the beginning? None of us can change time, but time certainly can and has changed me. Remember my disclaimer about absolute, OK? And no, it's not my favorite vodka either.

Or WTF. All my shit becomes void because of two bales washed up on sum beach? Wish I woulda walked. But didn't. Oh, well. Maybe next time. Maybe knot.

Chapter 19
Be Scene, Not Herd: In Lieu of Bud Rose

To the youngsters and to not-so-young people, I'd like to describe my true opinions about weed before we become a little too enamored with its allure. *Rule one*: Stay your asses away from it. It has a cumulative effect upon its users and, over the long term, will certainly render you not as effective or vibrant in this life as you otherwise would have been. That simple. "Total buzzkill, dude." I've noticed most broke asses tend to resort to "the buzz" in order to deflect the idea they are indeed stupid, lazy, or both. If you drink and smoke weed regularly, you're a useless slug with nothing to offer your family, and you are causing your mother high anxiety. Now there's some firsthand info. When you accentuate the physicality over the intellectual ability, you're a mere left-behind, nonevolving monkey scratching his swollen balls on that very same flappin' tree branch with some illusion that the opposite sex in your world is going around drooling over the instant fantasy of you. Embracing the idea that your stupid-stoned ass cluttering up their scenery is somehow the expected outcome. Get real. While allowing a degree of entertainment through stories of illicit activity, please do not construe these as stories condoning the concept of uselessness. The concept of uselessness is an easy reel and an unrelenting battle for significance. It's my obligation to inject some opinion here, OK? It's maturity to have reached this place, and you should know that any such older person should wish for younger ones to avoid inevitable pitfalls and have a better and more meaningful life. There is no particular reason for it. Just interaction with my everyday "peeps."

I personally would like to witness you successful and happy in this life. Just saying…this wish is far less likely to come true when you are twisting up hoggleggs and lounging around on your mommy's couch with the remote control in your hand, crunching back on your last bag of Doritos. I have seen this one hundred times: when people wake up with one of their primary ambitions being to twist up a fatty, they invariably seem to share the same address as their flappin' mother, "in-between jobs." And you can bank that shit in a permanent account. More likely to vote stupid, too, and there's the true essence of ignorance. A creed or cult, if you will, of ignorance. One in which nobody is offended and every stupid shit gets his day and his meaningless trophy. Be seen not herd. And hey, we are all stupid enough without weed, to boot. Fire the fatty up. I get it. Relaxes you. Used to relax me also. Used to smoke a little smoke, mostly to sample the payload or two. Paint yourself into a scene you may enhance one minute or whose course you may change the next. Weed has not the ability to serve you, you know. And you should damn certain avoid serving it. Or are you just plain stupid and all comfy amid the idiocy confirming all of us are united? Equally thriving while sharing the scene of misery?

Speaking of scenes, you just gotta discover yours. Critical. With the discovery of your scene comes the more likely easy path to contentment. And without your scene defined, you are five times more likely to seek a substitute scene with a buzz in lieu of it. Speaking of "in lieu of," here's a poem written while in solitary during my stay in the big house. Written for my dear friend DT. She's helped me stay sane and connected through the madness, even though disagreements abound in our respect for each other. I wanted to send her a present for her birthday, April Fool's Day, but couldn't due to the restrictive nature of solitary mailings. Thus the poetic justice:

"In Lieu of Bud Rose"
Man time ticks mysterious -- in waves which frankly hide
Obliquities sly earthly praise -- dark creature-faced inside
As frantic stuck on painted lie stained windows looked not in
Seize passing child through fire's eye like-minded beast within
Have finally booked occasion's choice the dream see I in hand
We trees of life seek wisdom voiced fed courage good of man
Outside this royal possession's cause young, promised eyes entranced
Jet streams alive the band takes pause - peculiar of them dance
Long answered ever questions sleep spare truth, some drink dimmed fool
A toast where feared twin eagles deep cheers none whose egos rule
But wait, she hissed no fool this day; the nerve forsake my birth
Mind yours I say I've missed say I for all time man-tocks worth.

Liquor, beer, weed, or other dope. Other dopes, too, in all their surefire contributions. Your scene awaits you. Its purpose and effort. Bank this for real, yo. Business and dope don't mix, unless of course, your business is dope. Even then, one should not mix the distributor and the consumer aspects. There're simply far too many ways to fail. Hear me, people.

The search for your scene is easy. Assess yourself. Should you be a people person—good with people, all these types of things—then maybe opening a dog grooming business might not be a scene well suited to you. It's sorta getting in where you're fitting in. Hey, do people tend to get on your nerves? Be a surveyor, a truck driver, or a landscaper. Not a janitor in an office full of busybodies. Whatever yours might be, should you drink twelve or more beers a day, waiting for the scene to reveal? You're dead after twenty-five years. Bank that one too. Then bury it. I've been to about five funerals of tough guys who were avid beer drinkers. Dead and stinking. Stupid and stiff. Would rather have a buzz than a life. Beats the shit outta me.

Chapter 20
Paging Earnie

Let's go down by the river and observe an off-load, shall we? It was the third of November; that day I'll always remember. 'Cause that was the day I just about shit the Depends. Again. This story is wild. I'd been in the business for a couple years and was very busy trying to find smuggles (boats loaded with weed needing a secluded place to off-load) that could use our family plantation. I showed the plantation—the off-loading area—to so many guys that after a while I was afraid some were using the occasion as a recon mission, to see where it was and simply avail themselves to it, or sell the off-load site whenever they wanted to without my knowledge, much less any payment this way. So I started charging ten grand to give the place a look. We called this earnest money simply "earnie." I collected several earnies. Just showed a few "what-ifers" (that's what I call guys that dream of being a smuggler—what if I can put a boat together? What if I can find a crew and get the thing loaded? Et cetera) and bam! Happy ten large. When they bitched about the fee, I told them, "Hey, if you ain't serious, then neither am I." Beat it. Ride your stupid ass out. A couple guys would bring interested parties around, guys I thought to be investors. They would throw down the Earnie, and I would never hear a word again. I found out years later that they were bilking the interested saps out of investment cash under the illusion of easy money, never having the intent to actually run the gauntlet. The royal scam was, as it turns out, only a scam. Simple as you fleece. Have to admit that the resourcefulness of the scam was quite creative. But true resourcefulness revealed itself as not having to deceive as a means to create. True resourcefulness revealed itself in a more positive manner through a couple of U-Haul rentals sitting there at the spot with eight tons of weed stuffed in the back. A good MF from back in the day, Willie the Hogg, is quoted as saying, "Every bale [of weed] represented a new BMW." So let's be aware of the payload, boys and girls. Shall we, please?

Anyway...and so the story goes, this one guy I showed the place to threw down his festive ten large and said his boat stuffed full of groceries was very close and he'd be in touch. After a couple of very slow, agonizing weeks, he contacts me and wants to come scope out the off-load site once again, you know...refresh his own recollection, bring the drivers of the trucks, and work out some basic logistics.

Well, we meet down there at the spot, and to my shock, there is a festive little garden of baby weed plants everywhere around the river off-load area. It's apparent some other group(s) have off-loaded recently and spilled seeds everywhere in their haste. There were clumps of busted weed bales all over the place. In the open. Hell, I wanted the guy to leave so I could rake up all the free shit. Not very professional and quite uninviting and unprofessional to the now somewhat and quite agitated what-ifer. Well...this guy became upset and started yelling at me for not keeping his "reservation" clean and open. I told him my partners must have sold the place and not told me one thing yet, and I was glad they told me nothing because not wanting to know anything to begin with. I honestly had no idea who had used it then or any of the other dozens of times. After all, we don't sit down there with a guard posted. As if. Hell, I spun it as a positive about how off-the-radar the place is. He didn't exactly buy it.

So to calm him down, I explained that we had another off-load site on the opposite side of the island (we're talking Edisto Island, just south of Charleston, South Carolina) that we reserved for "personal" off-loads and that he was welcome to it since the exclusivity of his plan A seemed to have been, shall we say, a bit compromised. At that instant he demanded to go see the other place. It was just across Edisto Island on Peter's Point Road, on the south side. And off we went.

May I recall to you people that I remember that drive down Peter's Point Road vividly? The freshly paved asphalt with the falling leaves blowing all around as we went breezin' by. Could the Calgon jet please take me away? Just me and the very nervous jacked-up dude who had thrown down everything he had for some long-shot pipe dream, his friends on the way with one of their dad's "stolen" fifty-five-foot sport fish. It was an all-or-nothing proposition for the poor guy, the crew, and just everything else, as it all depended on a secure off-load site. A good spot. 'Course I was so detached from his "I Have a Dream" speech on the way over there that I tended to focus instead on that one precarious leaf that somehow became lodged just in front of the star (the hood ornament) as we made our way down Peter's Point. Anything, please, to avoid having to assess the tenuous announcement in real time. "Hey, buddy, would you mind if we pulled over so I could maybe shave my ass with a straight razor? Would that be OK with you? Then we may be on our merry little way?"

We approach the gate at the very end of Peter's Point Road. We hop out and walk around the gate, walking the couple hundred yards and eventually arriving at the place where we would preview the dock area over on the right. Wow. What if someone's here? What if they have the gate locked 'cause they don't want any company? What if they just unloaded a few tons here last night? Hell, I don't know what they might have going on, not the foggiest clue. All these things blur my vision as we make our way up the short driveway. We break into the yard, and, thank God, the place seems deserted. There's a small camping trailer parked just yards from the entrance to the walkway down to the dock.

The poor guy naturally loves the place. Who wouldn't? Its *Prince of Tides* has an in-the-raw feel. Its seclusion. My assumed legit association with it seemingly securing the place amid the local vibe, illusion not included. To this day his question still rings in my ears: "Hey, Skippy, what's this camping trailer doing here?'

"Oh yeah...that camper." Hell, I didn't have the first clue about any camper. WTF does any camper matter? "You see, my cousins come down here from time to time and work on the house. You know...enjoy the river, fishing, hunting, and get a few repairs and renovations done also, and they stay in the camper especially when it's cold out, so they don't have to heat that huge house." Take a bow. It worked. My guy was stoked with the spiel and the feel of it all and told me to be on standby, that he'd be in touch. Wait till you hear the rest.

He was in touch, all right. About four hours later. I had driven back to Beaufort, South Carolina, to my mom's house; there I was trying to stop shaking and enjoying some macaroni and cheese when the damn phone rang, and it sounded like that jolt of an alarm ringing at the beginning of that song by Pink Floyd. Scares the shit out of you. This fellow said something to the effect of, "Look, man, the boat is almost here. We've directed a couple U-Hauls to Edisto down Peter's Point Road. We'll be expecting you within the next couple hours. OK, see ya. Bye." *Click.*

We've all heard the expression, "Be careful what you wish for." That scene in *The Wizard of Oz* where the four of them are walking down the hall and they enter the room where the wizard is? Remember the cowardly lion? Changed his mind in an instant, and after regaining consciousness, he ran down the hall and jumped through a window? Well, that was my big dumb ass. At this point I knew good and well we were gonna be busted, but for some reason didn't seem to give a shit. Hell, I'd signed up for it, I'd accepted money in advance for it, and there wasn't any turning back at this point. This point of no return. That same point of no return commonly referred to by pilots as they're taking off down the runway building up airspeed; there comes this place in their heads where if something malfunctions, they are trained to nonetheless proceed despite the malfunction, the reason being they have passed that point of no return where there's too much momentum and not enough room to try and abort or turn around.

Now all there is to do is follow through. Had to go there and face whatever there was to face. On the way there, I pulled into a store off Highway 17 North. Sort of a grocery and hardware store. Wood Brothers store. First on the agenda was to attempt to have a key made that might fit that lock securing the gate to the place down Peter's Point Road, where the dreaded trespass was to take place. I'd written down the number sequence on the underside of that lock and told the man at the key counter that it was a lock to a hunting club and that I lost the key to it. I asked if he could please try and fix me up with a replacement so I wouldn't look like such an irresponsible knucklehead to the hunting club members trusting me with their key. He looked in a couple of manuals and then etched some ridges on the key with his machine and told me it should work but that in the event it didn't, he had something that would. That something was a $120 three-foot set of bolt cutters, which I purchased as a backup. And off to Edisto, my journey continued.

Chapter 21
In the Meantime

And here's this. Not once has anyone ever come up to me and said, "You got exactly the prison time you deserved, you asshole, and the weed laws are totally spot on." Quite the contrary. So I'll write about what I consider to be the BS and why it is that most people these days seem to put up with such irrationality even when we don't agree with its underlying foundations, much less grasp the usual motives in play. Hey, as long as it's happening to somebody else, some other dumb shit, we'll go ahead and let it happen, I guess, right? We wear this mask not only concerning the culture of drugs and courts but more so the everyday hustle of the street, chasing us down in practically every single aspect and perception of life. Bending us all over, then bilking us all out of our dust, the entire time beating us stupid with the cult of celebrities and uselessness of nonstop entertainment. Any major dude with half a heart will surely tell you, my friend. Well, what do you know? Ole Skippy is a major dude.

After many years in prison, I can tell you everybody there learns to do the numbers as a matter of routine and survival. To profile. To summarize. To discriminate. All day, every day. Merely based on the truth of the real numbers about us. The odds. In the real world, decisions based on numbers afford us peace of mind. A fallback defaults to what's the real reprieve when the usual go-to ones invariably strive to deceive and disappoint. Emotional or impulsive choices tend to serve others better. Just like on the street. Ask your car dealer, tax preparer, doctor, politician, et cetera. We're all emotional creatures, you know, and I, for one, am happy this is the case. When your ass or your money is on the line, we should allow emotion yield somewhat to the numbers in play. But then…if sometimes you'd rather void someone's successes, which are usually based on numbers and on math in general, you're just a hard person.

This is not to say you should disallow a little space in your world for some balance. For some wonderment. Some of your own. But here's some raw emotion for ya and just a taste of what it's like at a sentencing hearing in South Carolina criminal court after my weed conspiracy trial in absentia and subsequent capture and return as I elected to ride the lam out in Reno, Nevada.

"OK, Mr. Sanders, I hereby sentence you to a mandatory twenty-five years and a twenty-five thousand-dollar fine. Is there anything you would like to place on the record at this time?"

"Yeah. You and these other state monkey jackoffs can kiss my skinny rank monkey white ass, and if there's anything else you wish to place on the record, call somebody wut gives a shit, as in *w-u-t*, MF."

"I'm holding you in contempt, Mr. Sanders."

"Hey, dick face, I was just sentenced to twenty-five years mandatory, which I can handle OK, but holy cow! Now a contempt charge? How brutal of you. Would those thirty days be consecutive or concurrent to the thousands I'm facing down already? Hold these in contempt, OK? Shove your contempt up your blowhole, then spray it all out upon that festive two-five mandatory, then carefully sprinkle that twenty-five large on top for emphasis. FokQ."

And with that, I'm carted away in new bling shackles and begin my 4,477-day ordeal amid South Carolina's degenerate elite. And sadly, while most of the above-mentioned exchange remains wistfully fictional, the 4,477 days in the big house were anything but.

Notable here is the very powerful dominion of a cult known more concisely as "illusion," whereby in this particular case, I sought to stroke some emptiness abounding with a ride upon that wave of illusion. My new illusion is now to offer a little insight in real-world bend-overs and to reveal to what extent you are being played for your cash while at the same time reminding us of our obligation to weave threads of civility with emotion throughout the course of our journey to maturation. Despite the road to enlightenment being one lonely walk, life is good.

What it boiled down to in my weed journey was simple. Effective law enforcement within the drug game depended primarily on two factors:

The easy and plentiful access to drugs, of course, being first and foremost, 'cause how the hell can a culture of opportunity through drug enforcement thrive without the damn dope? Anybody?

The creation and exploitation of propping up chickenshits to rat the world. Eventual flips. Well…sooner than eventual. Ask me; I know. uDam Skippy *W-I-N-O*.

And about that prison thing? Oh yeah. That part. In the federal system, when you are sentenced, they allow you to be on your merry little way, remaining on bond while they formulate a presentence investigation report, which takes a little while. Shortly thereafter, we file an appeal in federal court, and the Feds allowed me to stay out on bond during the course of the appellate process also. How nice. In state court? It doesn't come easy, not like round one. I was tried and convicted in absentia, and once collared out in Reno, Nevada, I was brought back for sentencing. That fateful day, once the sealed sentence was handed down, that was a wrap, my friend. My ass is instantly hauled away, and it's what you call *o-v-a*, baby, and that spells "ova." The first stop is back to a county jail; this one was in Columbia, Richland County. A quite festive little bivouac known as the Huger Street Hilton. A few days later, I'm transported to receive an evaluation at SCDC off Broad River Road, in Columbia also. I cried and wished my mommy were there. With some mac and cheese and a glass of sherry. Can I get a holy cow, Batman? A brutal forty-four days of bone-chilling temperatures and a mere sampling of the total buckets of shit I have been deemed worthy of spending the next twelve years with. My call. That's all.

Most of my preconceived notions regarding long-term incarceration that I discovered were, as with many other analyses on a variety of topics, incorrect. The lead-up to going to prison is itself the most frightening. You hear all these things, and you think, Oh my goodness, my ass damn sure can't sign up for that gig. And of course the big one is the rather large and dominating roommate named Bubba, whose favorite pastime happens to be chili dipping. So yeah, I was sweating the possibility of this being the case as well, and I can tell you every son of a bitch checking into a penitentiary carries with him these very same concerns.

Well, that's a misnomer, as it is 100 percent not the case. Say you're in a prison with 1,000 men, and out of those 1,000 men, roughly 150 are rocking horse people constantly craving more marsh mellow pie. They'll sling ass at the drop of a hat, sling ass for what they feel is a necessary hustle, or sling ass because they're on the fence and believe it's to their benefit to fall a little bit on the other side with ass sticking up in the stagnant air. As there are an additional several hundred souls as well, all too eager to exercise Mr. Happy, why would anyone go around and tree-jump an unwilling participant in the midst of dozens more than willing to entertain said stalk? My entire time in penitentiaries, I never once heard of a gang rape or a sexual encounter in any capacity, not to some degree otherwise known as consensual. It is puzzling to me that that lifestyle invites adulation and praise, plus, not to mention, is complimented by their very own special flag. How special. Sure.

I knew some of those guys and would sorta kid around with 'em, sayin,' "Hey, we straight guys have our own special flag too, celebrating our unique lifestyle."

And one of those poor souls asked, "And what flag would that be, Skippy?"

"Stars and Stripes, MF."

Which brings me to roommates. Usually the prison tries to pair guys up that won't cause the other any additional anxieties. Feds fully get the fact that we are not placed in prison TO be punished but instead are there as punishment. Not the case in state facilities, mainly because most inmate interactions are left to the lower tier COs. While the higher up guys, captains along with associate wardens and the big dawg, the warden in charge, focus more on day to day administrative protocols. Last thing they want is listening to a thousand guys bitching. Plus those upper end guys make enough money, to where they can't be bought off by any of us either. So I only offered temptation to bottom tier newbies. My intent was to do time comfortably as possible. To this end I limited my requests from most COs to food. But did receive a few cell phones through the three more trusted ones. None of whom ever having been subjected to consequences thereof. Didn't rat them either.

During my twelve years in SCDC, I had about six notable roommates, each of whom proved to be a reasonable guy trying to get through the ordeal, exactly as was the case for me. My very first roommate was my all-time worst one. Period. At Allendale Penitentiary, was indeed this hair back biker-type dude with one leg. Lost his leg in a motorcycle accident. Locked up for the murder of a woman who he hog-tied and strangled to death after a tortuous couple hours of her futile efforts, begging for mercy. We even talked about this briefly, and his explanation was something to the effect of "I told the dumbass not to struggle, that I was going to be right back and everything would be cool." Life meant nothing to this guy. The only thing that matters to such a psychotic bucket of shit is the perception by many other egomaniacs that they're indeed tough guys. The true badass. And instead of saying, "It doesn't have meaning," you have to say, "Don't mean dick." Well, this one-legged mook biker moron, I noticed the first night, did not seem to enjoy any association with black people, which I thought right peculiar for the entire prison system, which was indeed at the time, about 75 percent black. But old Poppa Crutch seemed hell-bent on the ridicule of these men for the simple reason his accident happened to be at the hands of an elderly black person driving the subject car, causing his injury. And I presume as a courtesy to a man having only one leg, most of the guys Poppa Crutch would go out of his way to insult seem to give him a pass due to the fact of his hardship and handicap.

One evening there was a knock on our cell door, and it was a very irate, insulted black dude who had had enough of Poppa Crutch and all his unnecessary antics. Poppa Crutch hops over to the door and opens it, and, lo and behold, the dude is standing there with one knee bent back to his thigh, secured there with a belt. There were fifty people on the rock cheering for this guy as everyone in there had grown sick and tired of my roommate's bullshit behavior. Now the odds were even. They both had only one leg.

"This is long overdue, MF. Bring yo crusty cracker ass out here and post up." My roommate begins to shake in a very cowardly manner and curls up in the corner of his bunk, fully exposed for the woof he was. He promptly checked himself into solitary confinement in the PC unit, which in this instance stands for "protective custody." It's where guys run to when they're scared of getting their ass beat, usually due to debt, snitch bitchin', or simply being an overall asshole, as was the case for ole Poppa Crutch. PC is considered very humiliating and is usually followed up by a transfer to another yard, where the story becomes that they transferred due to their being such an uncompromising "badass" and fostering mayhem.

The next two weeks were a glorious time for I had the cell to myself. Oh, for privacy. For sleep. For no traffic or any of the volatile scenarios liable to happen at any second when one is forced to duly associate with such a character as crutch boy. One day there's a knock on the door, and it's the same guy—the one with his knee folded up in the belt, holding it.

He said, "I hear you might be in the market for a roommate," to which I immediately responded, "Hell yeah."

He was a great roommate. He had converted to Islam on the inside and was a totally respectful guy. Easy to do time with, which is critical. Never on edge, never messed up, never any of the bullshit games. Damn near refreshing.

One afternoon after count, he said, "Hey, Skippy, I got a request of you—do you mind?"

I said, "Sure, go ahead."

He said, "The next time you need to take a leak, I want to show you something."

And with the slightest hesitation, I said OK. His name was Malik, and I noticed he was a superbly clean individual as are many of the Muslim followers.

When I said, "Hey, I gotta take a leak," he said, "Give me a minute." He placed newspapers on the floor all around the toilet, then said, "Go ahead." When I was done, he pointed out the hundreds of droplets of urine on the newspaper and asked if, in order to keep the area more sanitary, would I be willing to sit to relieve myself, just as he'd done over a hundred times. I thought it might be a medical condition but discovered why. In exchange Malik volunteered to handle the cleaning of the room detail. "Not nearly as dirty now; not a big deal."

To this day, guess what? I generally sit to piss. So what? As a result, me and my gal's bathroom is a lot more sanitary, and why not? Hey, just giving you a dose of the real scene. Wow, this is perhaps info you could certainly do without. I hear ya. However, it illustrates how one may acquire a new approach to a lifetime's routine. What? You're less of a tough guy because you happen to reside in a much cleaner area? My gal prefers cleaner. Good enough for me.

Malik was a fine guy. Honest. Rational. Word was good. A wonderful roomie for almost two years, but all good things must pass. He's in the top three of my all-star room-mates. The other two being Harry Eugene Claibourne, a federal judge from Las Vegas he was my very first roommate upon my arrival at Maxwell FPC in Montgomery, Ala. And number three is a man I speak of here a little more in depth later, ole Joey.

Malik and Judge Claibourne both were superbly intelligent gentlemen. Though practicing thoroughly opposite ideals through their religions, they both conveyed to us all the unprompted messaging many of us eagerly awaited to absorb every chance we got. Their ideals matched practically identical in terms of confirming our delight to share time amid such men of wisdom whereby both of them somehow found themselves in the company of us less intellectual types. As if... Hey y'all maybe we not as dumb as we thought. Here's a couple examples where these subject two seemed to jell:

They both proclaimed they believed our worse President to be Woodrow Wilson. And that our worst year as a country was 1913. For in 1913, four distinctive entities were formed or enacted. Surprisingly, they both believed the sequence of events occurring that year were not in the better interest of America.

The Federal Reserve, IRS, FBI, and the Anti-Defamation League. Puzzling, they both considered these entities the onset of our country's downfall. I, myself am completely void the compassion these two unrelated men shared, however the experience of posting up in a prison cell of all places and hearing this insight? Unreal. Still.

Which delivers me to rules. Prison rules. Personally? I could give a shit less about prison rules, or that I wasn't supposed to have a cell phone, or that I wasn't supposed to run a bookie empire (referred to as gambling and loan sharking). I cared about trying to live comfortably, as I was accustomed to living my entire life. My focus was trying to get through the ordeal and boomerang my ass back to the beach. uDam Skippy rules. There's a big difference between where somebody may think your ass deserves to be and where your mind actually is. The system had 100 percent discretion on where my ass was stored, but zero say where my head was situated. My message to my room mates (and to anyone trying to get through some prison time, known or unknown, or some other stressful times): is I wish all souls safe passage along with all sincererity. Keepin' it easy. I got the news both Malik and the Judge have long since passed. Both, my brothers in time. Neither one assailed the other's philosophy. It's rare these days trying to apply that statement in terms of some of those perhaps disagreeing with ours. Peace out.

My next roommate was a very strange character named Gatyam. A very quiet, short, dumpy sort of guy always kept to himself. He was locked up for arson, and we talked from time to time; it turns out he was homeless and lived under a bridge, and I think he may have committed arson for money. People would park a car nearby, and he would go set it on fire. The guy had to make a living, but as far as I could tell, that's kinda what he was in there for.

Much of my entire prison bid was spent running a sportsbook, and there were endless interruptions—people coming by and dropping off tickets. For this reason I was considered an A-rated roomie. Didn't smoke. Didn't snore. Plus the giving-them-something-to-do factor and the entertainment factor notwithstanding, me and my roommates feasted like kings due to the abundance of food supplied to me through the action in lieu of cash. My cellmates did the flying, and I did the buying. Same as it ever was. More or less understood.

To my dismay Gatyam opted out of this program. Flatly. Refused categorically to ever accept one bite of food (commonly referred to as a "setup"). In fact, he went so far as to refuse leftovers as I threatened to flush them several times when we were on extended lockdowns. It all got flushed. A real shame. He explained he was programmed to provide for himself, invoking the discipline default minus one iota of reliance upon anyone other than himself. He did not wish to void the mindset that allowed him total off-the-grid independence. He never once borrowed anything from anyone. Borrowing in the big house is the number one way guys become trapped off when expected money or other expected means to generate canteen items to pay debts back on time fall short. Shortly after the run, came a new prison transfer and yet another lucky draw in a roommate.

This one was named Joey. He was a quite articulate guy. He was the inmate preacher and choir director. One of the better people I have ever met. Anywhere. Stood six-foot-six. Three hundred and ten pounds. And not fat. I'd have to say that he was by far not only my favorite roommate but also a most educated and rational person, in my mind at least, hands down, in the penitentiary. He knew our religion exceptionally well as far as referencing or foundational aspects of traditional stories and documents we are all familiar with. His explanations seemed quite logical. May I say well-versed? Did I mention he was a black man? Just a man he was. The epitome, no doubt, of what MLK had in mind when he asked others to "Judge my people not by the color of their skin but rather by the content of their character." He taught me, likewise, that the very notion that if one hesitated to extend to all people a fair shake based upon mere differences, one would deny themselves initial association with such a sterling person like Joey. He defined resolve in his sincerity to assist others more prone to impulsive behavior and in offering up his own actions and wisdom as a genuine role model and mentor. And he was a role model for me, no question. His approach to being locked down and managing time as opposed to confronting time, helped all of us around him maintain a bit more sanity. To this day my gratitude remains strong for his allowing me to play guitar in the prison choir.

On those Sunday mornings in the visiting yard prior to visitation hours, I would many times be the only white person among the two hundred-plus black men up in there. To recall some of his sermons is mind-boggling, given his determination to project real-deal scenarios as they pertained to those in attendance and attempt to describe to these guys that they had to elevate their game to better conform within society so others might be more willing to freely associate with them. He described to the room that opportunity itself is not a guaranteed right, that it must be garnished from someone with the capacity to offer it, and in order to do so, one must present themselves in such a manner that the matter of trust within the association is viable. Through speech. Through how you present yourself. Through common courtesy and respect. Let me tell you one thing: respect is a big deal in the big house. A perceived episode of disrespect, whether or not actual, can have dire consequences. I have personally witnessed such encounters leading to death. Several times. Over fcuking nothing. Then instantly went to prison officials regarding such encounters despite otherwise past refusals to do so—to give information. And the prison never even took a statement. I wrote families of deceased victims and never heard back a word. Go figure.

Oh, I had several other roomies, but enough already of the nameless faces. Just as I was to them. The lesson taken from the various personalities I came to live with is simple: pertaining to the initial perceptions of prisoners in general, while prisons are indeed places where the worst of the worst end up, when one is closely confined with an individual—with damn near any individual—it is comforting to seek out the positives therein and, with a sigh of relief, realize it could have been a whole lot worse.

Chapter 22
Mandy for the Moment

Give me a moment, would ya?

When a kid nails that winning field goal or a chair or two spins around on *The Voice*, allow the numbers there and the rarity of those odds on behalf of that individual to invoke a toast of celebration in our cold, hard interiors. Moments define our lives, you know? All of us strive for recognition and significance, plus we all tend to reflect on and embellish such moments. To fall back and recall those times when we had our moments. Oh my, how we long for 'em. We were significant. We did have something to offer, to remember. There's many of them in sports. It's why we all love sports. The emotion of sports. Plentiful. We can all be part of it. I love it. Bruce called 'em glory days. Embrace those times. Thank God we live in 'em.

Take a minute and recall the top ten moments of your life. I bet you have some doozies. Here are a few of mine, just for the halibut. And how they directed my paths through turmoil.

Once upon a time, while on the lam out West in Del Mar, I was invited to a race track, and this guy apparently had access. We were standing a mere fifteen feet from a dozen race horses running flat out right up against the rail. Man. What a thrill. That sea of muscle. The pounding of the earth. The energy. I got to thinking of all the effort, work, and training that allowed this place and this instance to occur. Thousands of jobs. Millions of dollars. It all comes down to those dozen horses having been trained their entire lives to do just this one thing a mere fifteen feet away. And there stood me running hard and racing my lost soul. On the run myself. Flat out. Screaming to get nowhere. Maxed out with anxiety. But for these brief few seconds, a reprieve. Lost in the marvel of human endeavor. Incredible both then and each time it is dialed up. Now included. Check it.

The family had just moved to Beaufort, South Carolina. I am the goofy new guy at Beaufort High School. A big, intimidating school. Many Marine children there, so Beaufort High was in the loop. Diverse. Very hip. Other students assumed the same, that the new kid me in town was more of a worldly sorta kid, likely having transferred and traveled all over the place with my armed forces dad. There were guys there who seemed larger than life to me. Dressed cool. Had long hair. Smokin' in the boys' room. One guy had a hearse. Others had hot rods. One in particular, a '66 Chevelle 396, could pop wheelies in student parking. They had nicknames. A guy called Goat. My first black teacher too. Mr. Orage. Clued me in to tryin' to help me fit in. Was really diggin' this new Beaufort scene, man. So one day I went shopping at a head shop and bought some bell bottoms. Imagine my country ass in a head shop. Purple ones. Whaaaaat? Wondering around curious if any of the cool girls may had "blossomed" just yet. Never been that innocent in my entire life.

I didn't really know anyone, but I found out quickly about some totally cool guys there who were in a band called the Plastic Society. Sorta hung out with 'em to a degree when they would jam acoustically in the halls between classes along with dozens of other students looking on too. And one day I mentioned I could play bass guitar. Well, hell's bells, to my surprise, they invited me to their practice garage to come check 'em out.

"Just swing on by." And I show up there after school that day, and they say to grab the bass and let's jam. What? Just a second here. Man. Ray Kearns was the bass player and a really good one at that.

And all of a sudden he says, "Hey, I just remembered; I gotta go somewhere, so I'll be back later." The drummer was a super cool guy; no, super cool cat named Paul Jones, while the guitar player was named Steve Gibson. Paul Jones was kinda the leader and sported John Lennon round glasses and all that. Anyway, I grabbed Ray's bass and cranked it up; many people from the school were dropping by and witnessed my jamming with these guys. "Hey man, you know any Zep? Any Butterfly? Clapton?" "*Dazed and Confused*," it was. "In-A-Gadda-Da-Vida." "Badge."

And lemme tell you one thing…the next day at school, the word was out. Hey, man, that new kid jammed out with the Society yesterday. Hey, he's cool. And could play. I never thanked the Society for this moment. Especially Ray Kearns. It's in this new kid's top ten moment of life. All time.

Paul Jones said to me at school the next day in front of a couple dozen kids, "Welcome to the Society, Skippy." Unreal. I mean, Sherri Harriot was in that same loop. The first Beaufort crush. Plus, Paul Jones turned me on to a new band on the national scene: The James Gang. Joe Walsh. Thanks, fellas, for that moment. None of you guys had to do this. It reshuffled my entire attitude, latitude, and gratitude. It was so golden in many ways in my little world at the time. Remains so. Off topic a little, but high times and way overdue to express to you guys. My gratitude. Very real.

Here are a few incredible words I heard at a very young age on a couple evenings:

"Ladies and gentleman, The Beatles." Just plain wow. Then a few years later;

"The Eagle has landed." "One small step for man, one giant leap for mankind."

Think of these words. A couple lifetime game changers. Damn it man, if they don't bring a whisper to one's soul, nothing will. About the moon landing. How is it that our guys could pull this off? Push that envelope. Invoke such confidence. Check it now. Check it good.

And check this. You. Hey, man...you're alive. You're here, and you're now. Welcome to the Society. Even though this might not rise to the standards of a moment's moment, you still, nonetheless, have capacity. Have life. Wake up and live it. Have hope to discover another highlight worth remembering. OK? When I was sick and depressed and locked up, reflecting on some of my true moments, granted me solace. Worked wonders, ending the flow of teardrops. There were many. Just that longing to allow future moments to occur got me through some rough ones ongoing. And you can believe that one as bank.

Here's an awesome gift so granted, only made plausible through various nefarious exploitations starring the dreaded contraband. Once upon another time, I found myself on vacation with a very attractive young, skinny, rich girl named Mandy. Her family was part of the industrial sector out of Charleston, South Carolina. Ole school money. We're lounging on a beach in the Caribbean. St. Croix? No matter. Just sum beach. Sum wear. Had it in a bad way for this gal Mindy despite the one-way street she considered 'us' to be.

Anyway, drink in hand, feet in the sand—all that. Full disclosure. There may have been a little umbrella involved; can't disclaim any independent recollection for certain. However, I can quite easily summon up some images of quite a few other attractive types portside playing beach volleyball, two of whom in particular had a couple of guys shuttering fast-winding Nikon photos of them playing in the sand. Suddenly we look up, and these two lovelies stroll over to us and asked with an accent if we would please join them in playing some volleyball. They needed more people, don't you know? Did I yet mention they were topless? Spoke another language? Hell...they were real, live professional models or something.

This may be a good time to demonstrate another type of snitchin.' Known as "dry snitchin.'" It's when one rats for the sake of rattin' and doesn't actually receive anything in return for it. I've been every sort of snitched on. Never the one doing any of it, mind you, but the subject of all. Snitch-snitchin,' dry snitchin,' slip snitchin,' whodatday snitchin,' all of 'em.

Here's a dry snitch for ya, at the expense of a man-time gender betrayal. We have all heard how we guys sometimes rate women on a scale of one to ten? Yeah, sorta primitive for sure, but ever since the movie *10*, it seems like a not-so-serious beer drinkers' salute. That one-to-ten scale is based mainly on looks. Right? Well, there's another one. And this is the dry-snitch male gender one about to be revealed. It's basically known as the hottie one. Based on that same one-to-ten scale yeah, yeah, not very PC. Sue me.

Mandy knew about both of the scales and in fact asked me to give her my associated overall street number for her. In aggregate terms, as in, adding both the look one and the hottie ones together. Ole Mandy was about a seven on the looks one. And a solid eight on the hottie one. Her street number was around the mid-15s. She was cool with it, and she even mentioned her thanks.

"Wow, was scared you might say a lower number. Was hoping for at least a twelve."

We laughed and joked around about the couple of models too. No biggie, people. Just stupid fun. And FYI, there's the more crucial one to ten rating too. The one regarding brain power. Brain potential. Sense and sensibility. Social graces. This real one invoked when the chase sorta settles back to the real where compatibility may issue the longer term invitation. Whereas the relying strictly upon the vanity ones begins to seem rather stupid.

Well, after the invite for volleyball, Mandy sorta said nothing there, sipping on her drink, whereas my response to them was to say with hand motioning that I was sorta perched up there on sum beach with my lady friend here, but thanks for the invite just the same. With that, they walk away Renee.

Mandy grabbed my arm and said, "Hey, Skippy…are you kidding? Look at me, man. Picture this now…We're on one of the world's most exotic beaches. Agreed? Two of the world's most strikingly beautiful women just asked you to come play some volleyball. And you say no? Look at me."

Then she continued, "I don't wish to be the reason you said thanks, but no thanks to their request. For it would be a no you should always regret. Get your country ass out there and sling some balls around, would ya? Seize this moment for yourself, for you never know. We may never pass this way again."

Well, this moment herein, for me, was Mandy, my lady friend. Very cool, confident, and not at all concerned over the usual—my jetting off with some hottie model. Yeah, right. Yeah, as flappin' if. Nothing to do with any of that in Mandy's world. It was a subtle means, likewise, for her to convey that we were not headed toward "being an item" couple either. She guarded her freedom as its value was thoroughly recognized by her. We simply were not there to that 'couples' capacity. Just a couple of young people, rich and healthy, checking out the world. Oh...and about that rich thing? Hers was real, while mine was totally fleeting and fake ass. To be clear. But my friend made that moment for us both. Branded that memory in my skull. Cool gal. And every single day during long-term incarceration, for many years, I would relive this story. Revisit that beach. Every single day.

The lesson here is simple, people: just let it happen. OK? Get the hell out of the way and just let that shit happen. Throw yourself into the night. That's all. While it might not be for everybody and probably not for us in any world that I'm welcomed to, well, that day... it was for me, the taste of pure nectar. I was the "they." Chillin' with model babes on some exotic beach. Nice. Couldn't tell me shit that day. And when the going got rough later on down my rocky road? That beach dialed up my silly ass ebbyday. I said. It helped me retain sanity and recognize there's more than one line in any sand under the sun. Reinforce, please, my ability to remain separate from the usual dullard lives most accept so that a higher standard, my higher standard may be served up. But first it must be discovered. Drawing from the more festive times, that sterling moment served to substantially alleviate some of the overly stressful ones soon to appear, accepting it as nothing more than a blessing. The mundane in me has dissipated. And please, Lord, let me not thrive amid mediocrity. Grant me these highs then slap me silly; challenge me equally with the lows. Don't want the straight-line approach. Thank you very much.

The point is, allow your time to shine. And likewise, see your pitfalls as obstacles you are betcha by golly wow gonna overcome. Why can't you be the "they"? All I'm saying. Live it, baby. And why not? Its what life is for.

Had it bad for ole Mandy. Have I mentioned that yet? Thought to use a non-bothersome approach to win her over. So…I called her dad's office and made an appointment, at which time we met, and he said, "What's your name again? And what brings you here, Skippy?"

"Well, just wanted to ask you about the daughter."

He says, "OK, what about her? I hear y'all had a great time wherever it was y'all may have traveled to, and I felt better, frankly, knowing she was traveling with you instead of the usual helpless little friend she wanted to accompany her at first. And it's rare that any of her friends pay their own way. Appreciate that very much as well."

"Well, Mr. Mandy's Dad, I would request your permission to ask her to marry me."

"Wow," he says, "This is sudden. There have been several men asking for my blessing regarding Mandy over the past few years, most of whom struck me as being broke. You don't strike me as being broke or trying to reel my kid in for my money. So that being said, I wouldn't have an issue with your request. After all, you both are mature adults, and I appreciate the courtesy here, you know. It's up to her. Not me. Despite the formalities. You understand my kid was raised in an environment of privilege. Allow me to ask how you might plan to extend this lifestyle that defines her world. But before you get into it, let me show you a few things. A few things that represent my successes."

And with that, he proceeded to pour me a very small shot of scotch and escort me to his private upstairs office, overlooking the world he'd created. Very impressive. It was great, you know? We were talking and all. He was asking how his beloved daughter hadn't mentioned there being interest to the point where marriage between us perhaps on the table. And I confessed that he was correct simply intending to pursue his daughter only if he gave the idea his nod and full approval. I didn't wish to spend time courting her only to discover Dear Ole Dad was not down and dirty with the program. Hey, the man sorta warmed up to this idea and poured me another scotch.

"This is rather unusual, Skippy, but I kinda like it."

There were all these pictures on the wall of this man's life of business and powerful people he knew shaking hands with him or cutting new ribbons for newly built warehouses with him. Politicians, shakers and movers, even a president. He went on to explain that these pictures represented his continuing efforts to maintain his role as a provider and asked if, before we got into my plans for future security, should there be any questions.

Blame it on the few drinks? Maybe? Go ahead. Blame it on the boogie. I thought our meeting was going great. My hope to pursue the grand prize Mandy and be able to say, hey, your dad thinks it's a good idea for us to consider becoming an item. He even said he might approve of our getting married. How 'bout that? So I was feeling it a little. Maybe too 'a little.' After all, I had jammed with and been welcomed into the Society. So maybe there was room for a good time banter with the ole dad, OK? So when he asked if I had any questions, I said, "Well...maybe just one. A curiosity thing."

"Are any of those guys you have pictures shaking hands with you on your wall...well...might any of 'em have pictures of them shaking hands with you on their wall?"

This was not the question to ask this guy. I wasn't then—or ever will be for that matter—on this guy's level. Oh yeah? Not. My futile attempt at humor back fired. The question was posed sorta tongue-in-cheek, you know? The air instantly left the room. The meeting abruptly ended. Just sorta lost my bearings to crack jokes in the middle of such a topic as this. He kept his poise. Told me in no uncertain terms that he considered my judgment to be seriously lacking. He asked me to please leave. Get out. No point in future contact, and oh yeah...one more thing, stay the fcuk away from my kid.

He may have yelled out some parting shots as well, "You pusillanimous little punk fcuk."

And I know just what that word means too. Looked it up.

And that was that. Didn't contact Mandy directly again. Would see her out and about from time to time, and since we weren't ever an item to begin with, its doubtful dear old dad bothered to even mention my fiasco to her. My crash and burn to her. It was rather empty. Color me stupid as hell. Not everyone craves to be entertained. To Mr. Mandy's Dad, I was out of line. An apology is hereby formally submitted. You made the right call. Disregard the question please. We weren't buddies or anything. I should have read the room. It was gut-wrenching. Summarily dismissed, and rightly so with a serious overdose of both smartass and dumbass. The downside of overt criminal assumptions.

But hey, bottom line? A fifty-dollar photo opt at some political fundraiser didn't elevate this guy to running shit. It was all a front. There was no one with a picture on their wall shaking hands with this dude. Major or not. That's what pissed him off. He knew it. I knew it. A simple guy with good sense attempting to attribute his many achievements through some special considerations and connections of privilege. A rather simple man seeking explanation as to why he wakes up one day and discovers he is wealthy. Happens all the time. People such as Mr. Mandy's Dad bark out stock answers like, "It takes hard work." However, in the instant people standing in his office all googoo gaga impressed by such a person's successes? Employees and customers can't connect the few decades of struggles and of all the hard work required to achieve success. And sometimes neither can the people having achieved all this. Seems they – we -search for something too as to explain, "how the hell did I get here?" Thus, the pictures on the wall. Thus, a nasty ride or two. A tangible reason we little people may attribute another's clout and stroke as partially or mostly responsible for such successes. And... for the subject successful Mr. Mandy's Dad too. "Hey I guess that donation and photo op with ole Sperm Thurmond helped me win that state contract after all." Men like him ain't used to being called out.

Chapter 23
Show Me the Money

We've yet to talk about the drug money, honey. All the comradery, all the adventure, all the intrigue, and all that livin' la vida loco. Yeah, there was some money enabling all this fun stuff to happen. The money—we called it dust—made a lot of things possible that none of us would otherwise have been able to do. uDam Skippy was no doubt what is referred to in many circles as a small fish. A minnow. Indeed. But let me tell you one thing, I've been broke and I've been not so broke. A couple times over. Being with means is much better. The first couple hundred grand you make comes in sorta dandy handy. The transition from having nothing to suddenly being overwhelmed with an instant and what at the time you consider a practically unlimited flow of cash is something I dare suggest very few of us possess the actual ability to cope with. My ass sure as shit did not. One must avoid getting all goo-goo-gaga-batshit crazy or thinking you're some sort of big shot and that all this was destined to be. Or that lucky is the new smart. It ain't.

Now that I have finally become a true adult, having shed most of the frivolities of youth and unbridled risk, listen when the following is said to you.

The secret to money is to not set yourself up for a lifetime of limitations. If you want to be a teacher, if you wish to be a nurse—are you with me? A surveyor. Join the military, fire, or police departments? If you clock in when you go to work as a career, while you very well might easily discover the many other aspects of selfless service or achievement, from the strictly monetary standpoint, you will never know that freedom that money itself enables. While my encounter with such next-level free flow was very short-lived, the brief experience therewith served to open up a new horizon. There were now automobiles in the picture that didn't require a shot-putter's windup to slam the flappin' doors shut all the way. There were mi casas inside gated communities that came—you ready for this one—with a maid. Whoa. These times began to reshuffle my approach to money. The clue-in had begun.

Sure enough, similar examples run rampant everywhere you look. Me gotta guy that started mowing lawns and now owns a notable landscaping and sod farm. He didn't place limits on success. His mindset demanded steppin' out there on his own face. Give it that shot. Trade some of the risk and security of a regular-type job for the chance to tee it up on your own and hope there's some short grass to play off the approach next. There's a farmer whose wife told me on a recent vacation to Edisto that they risked over $400K to plant in the ground about 1,300 acres of crop. A few weeks later, she said, they got lucky, mainly with weather-related timing, and harvested and netted way over million clams. They risked most of what they had. They applied three decades' experience to the decision to let it all ride. Couldn't be happier for them either.

I have businesses these days and have benefited from having an easier access to money. Out the gate. To get jump started. Even so, real business and real success don't come easy. They require timing and persistence. They require discipline and sacrifice of some weekends, a lot of fun cookouts, and not attending every kid's soccer game. 'Course, the business itself might enable one to buy the van that hauls the kids around to the games. It's the ultimate rush to achieve success through actual work. Opportunity is for everybody. No doubt. But results? That one's completely on the individual. Try not to bitch when an effort or dream on your part falls a little short. That's life. You learn from it. You move on to the next chapter. Resenting another's success demonstrates pure ignorance. And if my ass can do it? Can pull it off? Well, so can you. Through actual work, there is no having to look back over one's shoulder. There is nothing like it. Making money is by far the best drug out there. There is extensive research regarding the prior statement. So true. If only. If only coming out of the big house somebody would have given me a job? Didn't happen. I had to create a job. There was no plan "B." Turns out rock bottom has a basement (A sticker we sell. So true). I went to the basement and pondered life. Scratched ass. And decided I gotta go all in. it worked.

When my best gal says, "Get in the truck, you crusted up convict Bowinkle," why, we hop our asses in the cab, and off we go. What is this worth? A lot. Let's not forget that success requires a rock. My gal is a rock.

Smart and organized. No use in extolling her ability. She's not greedy at all. It's called ambition. Doesn't dwell upon the popularity she may or may not project. It's focus. It's organization, and it's consistency. The rest shall fall into place.

My biggest payday in the weed game was $600K in two days. Wow. Six hundred and ten thousand clams, to be exact. In forty-eight hours. What's left? Hell, that should be enough, right? I sat there with a couple suitcases full of twenties as the two guys from Canada bought over two thousand pounds of weed. And they promptly stuffed it in the most conspicuous tinted-out-windows black jacked-up knobby-tires van with Quebec tags and drove off north on I-95. A couple thousand pounds of the fine Colombian made that night indeed a wonderful thing. And they made it to their home and wanted more.

Now what? Where would you stash that kinda coin? We already know the numbers on it. About seventy-five pounds of dead weight. I did the deal in Yemassee. Placed the chunk with a loud thump in the trunk of the staff car, and what…mosey on back to Beaufort? Scared to go to the Batcave, where a LEO had already warned me a raid was imminent. Instead, checked into a motel room at Point South where you park just outside the door. Here again, I didn't tell anyone about the deal. No use gettin' hung about. Went inside the room and collapsed on the bed. Exhausted. Scared to call anyone. Scared to go anywhere. Had no place to go. The point is that all this free-flowing druggie money was nice. It was fun making it. But it was torment dealing with the bulkiness of the cash itself. That was why it was easy to freaking spend it. To take everybody to dinner and suck back six-packs of Dom. The truth was that cash was the burden. It wasn't real. It wasn't earned. I had zero respect—zero regard for it. Can it please just be gone?

Well...turns out most of it was gone. Infused into our public, monetary, and commercial grids. All of us gentlemen smugglers injected a shitload of liquidity into our local economies. You notice these aspects of weed slingin' dare not ever be discussed or even mentioned by state actors. This single jackpot episode consisted of over $600K of out-of-state money that I personally and substantially bolstered our local economy with. Smoke that one. And so true. Tax free, just as authority would proclaim (i.e., "not paying their fair share"). All that rubbish. That all being said, all of us were having local guys build rooms and porches or other improvements to various homes. Buying new cars and appliances and electronics. Hiring landscapers and maids and having nonessential dental work performed. Booking vacations through local travel agencies. We all spent a major chunk on local shops of every variety and countless restaurants. Beaufort County likely benefited from tens of millions of dollars of spending over the years. And as mentioned, though this money was tax-free to us, every dime of it was taxed at every level—many times over—down the line.

There are more numbers that we need to calculate as well. Many uDam Skippy types injected hundreds of thousands of dollars into various communities. However, when—which is full-time, BTW—government workers prefer to seize the initial chunks of cash as their own personal gains, they can't very well dwell upon in public the actual positive effects this illegally created money had on overall benefits to the many in the community.

There were many as it was indeed major-dude cash, people. It benefited, to a quite significant degree, nearly every business in every single community offering a service or product on which weed slingers might choose to spend their lavish harvest.

And speaking as a legit business owner today? I wouldn't give one shit less between two flushes should a group of people come into Coots Bar on Edisto Beach and throw down a few hundred in weed-generated bucks on a tab. Neither would you. No one I ever spent a dime with told me they didn't want that type of "tainted" money. Including lawyers, who never would ask, never did ask, "Hey, where did you get this Crown-Royal sack of twenties from?" In fact, attorneys turned out to be one of the safest places to dump cash. "Attorney-client privilege," they all cried. As a sidenote, they had it made with me, for mine was also "client-attorney privilege." Two-way street, baby. Never dropped a dime on any of my several attorneys, though a couple of 'em assume otherwise given that I received visits from Feds in prison. The Feds wanted to know how much lawyers were paid. Sorry, boys. You're in a no-rat zone. All it was about was Fed boys hoping for more free money. Anyway, in many cases, even when the Feds knew details of cash attorneys would receive, law enforcement would allow the attorneys to just keep it. Why? Because one day, there's a chance this particular prosecutor is gonna be in private practice, charging drug defendants based on the druggie's ability to pay, as they all do. And holy moly. These ex-prosecutors shall expect the same courtesy from the new prosecutors coming up in a like manner. It's a huge business. Zero risk to them.

Plus—and this is a biggie—say you're a druggie and more comfortable were you able to basically wash a few bucks and lessen the need to scramble should SHTF. And suppose you retain a notable lawyer to "defend" you and slip him $500K, as a retainer. Where if the so called retainer not invoked, there were honest attorneys that would and did a couple times, reimburse those funds. Very safe keeping. For an extended period; for a small fee of course. That's $500K in cash basically being protected. Even though it's vanished for the instant, I would ten times rather donate it to or risk it with lawyers-in-love than to have said chunk exposed to government. More incentive for you to throw down loosely when it comes to any attorney's "cut."

Chapter 24
Soft Intro to JJ

Speaking of the weight of money losing some bulk, another thing—only a fun thing this time around—one could invest practically unlimited illegally gotten gains in, was, and still happens to be; aircraft. A pretty safe way to invest a chunk, for the simple reason that not very many people ever put eyes on airplanes. It's not like you drive them around to happening clubs and park in VIP slots out front, steppin' out as if the world isn't taking notes. So yeah, there were keys to an airplane or two in the world of uDam. Along with an emphatic word of caution here. Just because the aircraft in one's dominion and control in no manner of speaking were any such skill crucial to operating the bird included. In fact my instructor guy, a superbly intellectual man and pilot, constantly preached to me just how much of a nonpilot I was. As I was one of his first students, he did not want me to blemish his flawless record, reflecting that safety was and still is his primary objective. I gladly complied with his incessant preaching, given that tarnishing his flawless record would likely mean death. Yeah, mine.

The instructor guy explained it to me via the following paraphrasing: "Since you seem to have more discretionary cash these days (i.e., allow me to observe how you enjoy playing guitar and how you have recently amassed several very nice high-end guitars), please keep in mind that no matter how many high-end instruments you might purchase, they do not have any correlation with your ability to actually play them.

"The same—times ten—may be said of any and all aircraft you, from time to time, seem to indicate to me you may consider purchasing. With dire consequences. You are hereby forbidden to fly anything unless you first notify me personally, and expect me to accompany you each and every time for the test drive. And whatever the hell it is you're smoking that somehow renders your vivid imagination, when it comes to aviation, that you're a real pilot? Wrong again, Batman. What's real is that you, my friend, are nothing more than in the fcuking way. Can you say that, Skippy? In the fcuking way? Keep your WTF fantasy lalaland pipedream the hell outta people's way. Are we clear?"

"Yes. Sir. We are clear, and not for takeoff."

We all can use a guy like my instructor guy. To this day I regard his instruction in the highest esteem. And after my more recent purchase of a nice little Cessna 182, he was part of the intervention of those dissuading me.

"Let's not go there again, OK?"

In addition to his objections, there were those from the brothers of my best gal, Swambo. Subsequently, the aircraft was given back, and with it, my dream of flying around amid our society's incredible ability to do so, DOA. Just driving around now instead, trying to stay out of people's way on highways too.

Speaking of airplanes and a trusting illusion of skill, a short time later, I received a call from Hilton Head's equivalent to Atlantis Morrissette, the lovely and gracious Ms. Joanster. "Hey, Skippy, whatdoyasay we meet at the airport in thirty minutes or so? Hop in one of your little free birds there and breeze on up to Atlanta for lunch? The thinking here is that cute little Saratoga we had lunch in the other day, remembering you taxied it closer to the tree for shade? Why, that one would get us there just fine."

What could I say? No? Well, an hour later I met Joanster down at HHI Airport and threw down the following cop-out: "Well...it appears the instructor guy has that free bird booked for a charter." Liar, liar pants on fire.

She said, "OK, then. We'll simply thumb to Atlanta instead and then grab some lunch like we planned. That cool?"

What the hell...a few minutes later, I looked around for the star of the show and heard an FBO guy say, "Yo, man, I ain't never seen nobody try that shit before."

She's got her thumb out on the taxiway at the flappin' airport! And you wanna know what cool is? What confident is? Picture that. One of the defining images I carry with me from those days we affectionately refer to as heydays. Another top ten moment of this life. No question. A beauty and sass of a woman with her thumb out on an airport runway? Needless to say, she stopped traffick there, too, and very soon we were off to "wherever you're going" in a sporty little Mitsubishi turboprop high wing. Pretty girls do indeed…just seem to find out early how to open doors with just a smile. With just that smile. Oh, so true. Turns out the plane belonged to a country singer, and off to Charlotte we were soaring amid the miracle of these times for a little lunch. Maybe next time Atlanta.

Take it all in, people. Liberty is a wonderful thing, and what is derived from it is even more so. This place. This time. To soar in the clouds for real and toast my own love of life face-to-face with the infinite sky and the invisible truth of God granting us a taste of these types of ungodly abilities. The miracle of us. What are the odds, to live and breathe in this time. To exist as chosen and cradled by forces so incredible to all able to fathom it. Hurling through the sky at 240 knots, finding it difficult to keep emotions in check, knowing we have it better than billions before us, including royalty of bygone eras. How could this be? A lowly slug like me living like a kingly cotton buyer of old. That a noble, humble, long-haired, leaping gnome should be gliding with stars as if in some scene out of a Hollywood movie, good on the very first take—somebody pinch me. Smack! Snap out of it, would ya?

"Breathe deep, Skippy, the gathering wings of these breaths for you a mere dog's back amid new angles; the sun itself seeks to shine but only for this moment's lull," cries my somewhat cynical pal. Again, in times of depression or hopelessness, we tend to reflect on those better times, which, for me at least, bolstered the hope for hope itself. Another flashback to that very moment in this instance. It never gets old. Mongo only pawn in the game of life.

Chapter 25
More Antics from the Joanster

Permit me to further introduce you to Ms. Joanster. Total box office draw. Such the everyday pretty girl from Hilton Head Island (HHI), who was in advertising. I bought some ad time from her network just for the sake of having a reason to be in her company. Personally having no business as such that would occasion the need to utilize a radio-formatted ad campaign, I opted instead to utilize newly acquired nightclub owner friends on HHI who didn't mind if I wanted to pose as part owner and promote their club. Not at all. Especially given the fact that not only were extended to them thousands in business revenue and sent them many thousands more, but I was now longing also to contribute to promoting their gig. Free (as in not "for free," but just plain free). So the lovely and gracious Ms. Joanster assumed there were some connection to a nightspot or two due to the VIP treatment everywhere extended to me, whereas I was granted the coveted "time of day" in her clock shop, where time was indeed on my side and seemed to become quite still. After all, she was in the biz of selling promotional packages. As any major dude will tell you, even the losers get lucky sometimes.

Ms. Joanster was very educated and very much the intellectual type. Very trusting in general yet a bit standoffish in the face of the free-flowing cash, though mine knowing all too well that the Benjamins were indeed the gateway to her peculiar inner visions. Oh, to be young, healthy, and rich. All sorts of rich. The Joanster generally sported around in the Birkenstocks; don't cha know…that sorta babe. Tall enough to pull it off, exactly what God had in mind when he created the first Ms. Joanster—yeah, that one we have come to know and revere as simply, Eve. It was about a shared commonality. Let's cork a bottle of red. About culture, music, expression, and the flood of nuances therein. Flying to Atlanta for lunch or allowing other impromptu trips upon whimsical review. Car, plane, train, or boat didn't matter. Never many questions. You go around once so…let's go 'round. Can still hear the phone call: "Why not? Let's ride."

The Joanster thought of me as some sorta trust-fund baby or something. As Hilton Head flush with many. No clue about my involvement in an illicit culture of bringing it in and slingin' it out. Whereas her world was an open book: a radio personality with a very public face out and about on the town. Hardly one somebody craving a lower profile would choose to associate with.

Consequently, on those occasions when an out-of-town trip would present itself, it was always the default setting in my book. To get away.

On one such occasion, I was delighted to announce receiving an actual invitation from Charleston to dine with some friends of mine, and friends I wished to impress, no less. So when they said you of course may bring a date, quite naturally the Joanster received an exclusive invite to accompany yours truly as my date for the evening. She said yes. Yeah. She said yes. And dats a'ight wid me. And so on the breeze-up to Charleston from Hilton Head, which is a touch over a two-hour run, we discussed our status in her mind as a couple, whether or not we were, in her words, still just dating? Or did I consider us onto the next step, officially as "seeing" one another. A bit later in life, I figured out the differences there.

Anyaway, we arrived in Charleston, fetched a trick little room in a downtown bed-and-breakfast, and proceeded to get ready for a night on the town as I checked in with my guy host, who extended to me the particulars. He said this was more of a meet-and-greet function than it was a dinner as there would likely be some people in attendance who were up-and-coming business types who one day would likely run this city and, who knows, might even offer up some investment opportunities for us both. "Plus, I thought to invite you because frankly this party is going to need some livening up, if you know what I mean." Yeah, I sort of knew what he meant, as known druggies are expected to have access to drugs and certain dealers on speed dial. Why the hell else would he want my crusty ass in the mix to begin with? Just being real.

It was wintertime in Charleston, and the temperature was in the low to mid-forties. We were all going to meet at 82 Queen for a quick toddy in the bar, then be seated in a secluded, private-type dining section. It was my favorite restaurant then and the go-to hangout for most big boy drug smugglers. Faked that one too. But 82 Queen? Still in my top three all time and hands down the best place for anything "crab" to this day. My favorite kingpin; Flash either owned or bankrolled the place and told me it was cool to go there and park any 911 right out front, and for those about to rock, we flappin' salute you. That's right. uDam Skippy knew somebody, and the staff knew Flash was my buddy and didn't ask any questions as they were quite poised to accept my Benjamins as tippage. All righty, then. So money can't buy you happiness. True. But that night it bought me a big fat yacht, big enough that you could pull up right beside it. Thanks to ole David Lee there for those eloquent words of wisdom.

Well, the happy couple arrived in timely fashion, and, big surprise, the Joanster looked like a million as usual (a valuation somewhat on the low side). We zoomed up to the parking spot just across the street from 82 Queen, and she pointed out to me, "Hey, liquor lips, you shouldn't park here. For one, there's a fire hydrant over there and maybe even a handicapped off-loading zone."

She asked, "Can't we just go park in that big parking garage directly across the street like everybody else?"

"OK, but we are running just a little bit late if we do that." No biggie, right? No biggie indeed. So we zip on up to the fourth floor and park the damn thing, and off we go. I am kinda hustling along, hoping to inspire same. Well, who would have guessed? Gimme three steps. Please? Just before we are about out of the place, I look around, and there's no Joanster. Figures. Can't take her anywhere. Let's call out for her. Hollering, "Hello, we gotta step it up; where did you go?"

Time to backtrack in the garage a bit, and, lo and behold, I find her squatting down next to this seemingly homeless person covered with the evening news; she's holding "this creep's" hand while encouraging him about how his hard times are soon to pass and how she feels his pain as this poor ole fellow laments, "Hell, lady, I was just tryin' to weave that dream again climbing out of my favorite tree, and further, I don't have any pain. Fatigue, maybe, but no pain. You don't know me at all. OK? Lets keep it that way."

The man wasn't particularly dirty or scruffy looking; he was just sorta sitting there on a couple of discarded Maytag cardboard boxes. I guess everyone enjoys a little hope, you know, and my thought was, this guy's situation is on him. Not us. She later suggested that sometimes she held my hand too and asked if that gesture was a misconstrued one likewise. Good question.

"Come on. OK? Can we please just get there? Can we show up sooner than later?"

She responded to the effect by saying, "Yo, man, if you looking to show up, perhaps you should've invited somebody else. I'm more of the 'arrive' type."

Never forgot that one either. Anyaway, we proceed across the street and are promptly whisked into our private little quarters where the rest of the party is socializing. Well, maybe "socializing" is not the apt description to capture this essence. Let's go with "competing," or better yet, "ordering another drink and not giving a shit if we show up or arrive or not." At least my friend was happy to see me and needless to say, somewhat impressed by my company. And by my company, I mean the girl whose black dress was power sliding its way around some seriously wickedly dangerous curves. Duh. Every head in there took a swivel. Not sure but could have been a few who were begrudgingly nudged or maybe even politely smacked.

We're all introduced, exchange a few pleasantries, and begin what's anticipated to be a nice, civilized dinner with friends. The pretender. That's me. To be legal. To be with means. Sporting an actual girlfriend. All of that is most enjoyable, but all of a sudden, the record needle scratches across the record my friends.

When the main course is served, the Joanster asks to be excused, clutching her plate of food, and heads for the door. My buddy's looking at me all like, "WTF? What is she doing?"

"Hey, be right back as I'm sure there's an explanation."

Well...you guessed it. She's back at the homeless site, offering the man her plate of food, which, to our surprise, he flatly declines. So she gathers the plate back up, and off we go to a second grand entry into the little room, where awaits my befuddled host and his table of several couples longing for some sort of explanation, just hating and hoping something is amiss here with Little Miss Can't Do Wrong, for all her vanity. Please, please let her just gimme some kind of sign, girl. Some flaw to diminish that glorious first impression, please. Lo and behold, a whack job, maybe? Or batshit crazy would be nice? Or, oh yeah, how 'bout a hooker on call? Anything. There were some strong women in the mix that night. A few poised for power yet to come in support of their men, likely throwing down the main rule my current and last and best gal came at me with out of the gate as being nonnegotiable.

And this rule would be, "Ain't but one bitch up in here."

A certain confidence men find difficult to resist. Count me as one, for sure. Anyway, amid the shrugs and facial expressions reflecting the puzzling candles exposing undeniable condescending superiority complexes, the sharpest gal in the room delivered a few thoughts of a very poignant nature off the cuff; no doubt the capacity itself most found rather disappointing, while others were quite impressed once she kicked it in, including me. Paraphrasing here:

"Please allow me to introduce myself. My name is Joanie Jackson, and I'm from Hilton Head, South Carolina. I work in the advertising business for several radio stations. I'm here tonight through an invitation from a friend of mine, ole Skippy here, as we like to get away from our island every so often for a chance, you know, to regroup, to ponder, and to reshuffle. As we arrived here tonight, on the way into this fine restaurant, there was a seemingly homeless man living, at least for this night, under a stairwell on a couple of discarded Maytag refrigerator boxes. Having never seen anything like this in my life before in person; I only heard that in some cities this condition may be considered a crisis. Perhaps he's the only homeless person in this town tonight, and perhaps I'm out of line to bring it up in such fine company or to the gracious host making this grand occasion possible. But I just could not, in good conscience, be part of a two-thousand-dollar meal, pretending to savor the moment, knowing there's a fellow human being less than one hundred and fifty yards from here, sleeping on a GD discarded Maytag refrigerator box.

My intention is not to create a scene with you fine people as I consider myself fortunate to be a part of such a gathering. However, I wish not to compromise my humanity in exchange for a bowl of the best damned she-crab soup I've ever tasted. And again, meaning no disruption to what this gathering may be about as it's not my scene to create a scene, but once the entrée arrived, the preference for me, the conscience of me, compelled my sporadic action.

Despite the homeless person's predicament, likely of his own choices and of his own standards, I nonetheless so elected to respond. Indulge me in respectfully pleading for your forgiveness, as to assure you there will be no further disruption. Please don't hold my actions against my guy; perhaps I should've just sat here and tried to look pretty and kept my pie hole shut. The homeless man refused my gesture anyway. Shows that my attempt to identify another's definition of pain was probably out of line. As was the disregard for the present company at hand. I'm quite sorry, and please, Mr. Waiter…could you kindly cork another couple bottles of Dom? I could use a drink."

Nothing fake about this gal. The brightest person at that table. The classiest woman there. The best looking one there. The most independent one there. The only one there not relying to some degree, some man to prop up her prestige. She didn't barter with anyone's clout except for her own. She was and likely remains independent and doesn't need to. It's nice to be wanted, don't ya know? For she needs nothing but independence created from within. Box office.

For all you needful sweeties out there, chances are Dear Ole Dad did you no favors training you to depend on others and that you are basically seen and rendered as helpless.

Which delivers me to the review of all four of the main gal characters in my life. Well, what do ya know? All were unmistakably independent. Otherwise they would not be or have been my gals. Easy enough. The current one is the last one. The result of my life's discovery is the fact that each person gets exactly and ends up exactly with what they settle for. To this end, one can tell much about a man with a simple assessment of the better half. Check out the wife. Check out the husband. The purest reflection of the other. Bank that. My search is hereby *o-v-a*. Golden.

More necessary lessons from the lovely and gracious one. Oh, the times we're missing spending the hours reminiscing. One afternoon amid my living the dream and breathing the fantasy of one lovely and gracious Joanster, I had the occasion to hang out with some of the boys for a little happy hour. Informing my gal that a comic performing at our nightclub happened to know a celebrity Association player who was in town and invited this comic with a few friends to meet him and his golfing buddies for adult beverages at the Dollhouse. Well, the Dollhouse happened to be a place that mostly men patronize and where they watch professional ladies perform to music. A more apt description may be a place that pervs frequent to drool amid other drooling pervs directed at hookers stripping and squatting by a pole. Mentioned this fact to my entertainer friend in the connection with the invitation: "Hey, man, I'm sort of seeing somebody now, so you suppose we could meet at a regular bar or a sports bar or Reilly's or Remy's or someplace like that instead?"

To which he replied, "My Association pal tends to draw an overwhelming amount of attention in public and can't seem to enjoy so much as a second's peace. However, at strip clubs, he seems to have immunity from such harassment and may enjoy a cigar and a beer without the usual and relentless interruptions. Guess you could say that that 'I am woman; hear me roar' thing supersedes the attention span of even one of the most recognizable sports celebrities in the world."

So with that seemingly logical explanation in my pocket, there proceeds me to inform the lovely and gracious one of my plans that early evening to join the boys for a couple of beers down at the ole Dollhouse. To which she responded, "Well, I suppose a couple of cold ones down in the old watering hole with the boys can't be all that bad...guess we'll hook up after the 'couple of beers with the boys' session is completed. Just gonna read the articles, right? No big deal, right, Skippy?" Ahhh, right. Yeah. No big deal.

This was pretty cool. Gotta great gal that holds on sort of loosely and allows a lifetime's shot to hang out with a famous athlete. A gal that trusts me enough to know I'm not in the game of chasing around empty skirts. And she's right. This occasion simply to be amid a real-life Association star while at the same time perhaps promoting the business to some degree by being attached to this celebrity, based on however some stargazer might correlate the two. And yeah, I was in awe to see this guy just being the guy. Talking about his golf game. Cracking a few jokes with our headliner for that week. Not the first whisper of ego at all. Was really sorta cool.

Down on the corner, out in the street, Willie and the poor boys are playing "guess who we got to meet?" So we're just chillin out, simply wanting to be seen.

"Hey, Skippy." One of the guys with us taps me on the shoulder. "Check out that fancy dancer up there...isn't that the Joanster? Your girlfriend? Holy shit. Is it her? What is she doing here up there dancing?"

This can't be. My gal is no stripper. There is a light in your eye, and then a guy says, out of the car, long hair. This can't be. My radio sales executive is in a place like this, dancing to Led Zeppelin's "Stairway to heaven?" Holy cow. She's a really good dancer. Dammit man. She was refusing tips from men trying to stuff bills in her garter.

My guys are commenting, "Hey, Skippy, your gal is one of the best dancers we've ever seen! She is nailing it." And she was nailing it too. Complete with an air guitar. Let the hair down. Whoa. Well, she continued this sterling performance, and as the song and Mr. Plant approached the conclusion, "And she's buying the stairway to heaven," my newly discovered gal eased back up the spiral staircase to the dressing room of this club.

And all of a sudden, all the guys at the table now know that's my sweetie and are giving me high-fives as if I just hit a home run or something. Even the celebrity in our company shot me a thumbs-up. And a wink.

About that time, here comes Joanster, dressed back in streets, approaching our table in a semipanicked half trot, whereby she proceeds to seek me out and plops down right in my lap with her arms and face about my neck. The adulation from the others around us seems to fade within the next set as she looks at me while describing this scene.

"This life in this place with these people is not for me. I know you are here today only in a social gathering capacity rather than as an opportunity to celebrate a culture such as this, one that lacks substance. True. While my business advertises this establishment, it's not a business in agreement with my values. So…here's my deal to you right here, right now. If you comfortably may accept this culture despite it's premise, then so can I, provided we accept it together. We'll just sell our souls, I guess. However, my preference is for us to continue our lives minus the acceptance of a culture such as this, whereas my invitation to you at this time is to take my hand. Let's walk our asses the hell out of here with the notion that we are secure and content with a life together minus the wretched excesses of a relationship. One involving lost souls believing they are somehow defined by degeneracy. What say you, Skippy?"

uDam Skippy. With that, I said my goodbyes to the fellas and departed the premises hand-in-hand with a woman more insightful and beautiful than ever. Very proud to this day, decades later, to proclaim to you directly that that episode was the very last time my ever setting foot in such a place. Thank God for the wisdom and goodness bestowed upon and unlocked for me that fateful day. I hereby challenge you to discover it as well. On your own terms. That women are not here to GD entertain us. That virtue is defined by character not by lust. That we are family and should regard each other as equals through faith and opportunity. That all the vanity shit being smeared in our faces is no substitute for truth and value of word-up. It's gonna hit you one day, and on that day, for me, it did. After all, I'm not anything resembling perved-up lower-tier Square Ds seeking such fake-ass escapes. By their very nature. My very nature dwells in a complete forest. And it's all owed to the good graces of one little ole advertising executive they simply call the Joanster. To my rescue. Thank you so much, JJ. You're one in a million.

Chapter 26
Why They Call Agents Special?

There were two really close calls in terms of actually being busted with weed. The first and potentially major one was referenced a little earlier, going to another potential off-load site with one of those what-if-fer Earnie type dudes. Remember our drive down Peter's Point Road and our pulling up to the place? In my description of the scene, there was the locked gate. My total apprehension. And as we arrive, the guy is questioning me about a camping trailer set up very close to the docks. "Yeah, right… belonged to the owners who come down here to fish." Well, we offloaded that sport fish the next night, which happened to fall on a Monday.

After the off-load, I contacted the owners with the intent to pay them something and determine if they were possibly interested in further involvement. The guy told me right there that he was already involved due to his leasing the place to the Drug Enforcement Agency as a field office and that they parked their mobile office camper by the docks and performed random patrols and surveillance from that location on a regular basis. You understand what this means, right? We unloaded a boatload of weed beside a DEA substation six feet away from the activity. Unreal. Came to discover, the shift agents took a break that evening and were in town at Applebee's watching the Monday night football game. Drink up, fellas. So yeah. This was pretty much a very close call. This off-load was one of very few never known or charged through any indictment or referenced in any DEA 6 material reviewed by me or the legal team.

The second close call came under the scrutiny of Big Stupid (the name I gave a state drug agent). Big Stupid had a hunch one fine day. His gut this fine day was, for once, spot on (not to be confused with on the spot). The Feds wouldn't dare grant this slug any sort of access pertaining to big boy drug activity. Smuggling. He was relegated to chasing small-town clowns around like me. This day he was following me on a correct hunch—a festive big boy sack of weed was likely in the back of a borrowed jeep. A mere head stash. In the open. 'Course, and thankfully for me, not only was said agent a couple fries shy a Happy Meal, but he also defined the epitome of a true chickenshit to boot, for his stupid ass was too scared to pull me over by himself, so he peeled off, calling for backup or maybe shivering in the corner somewhere, much to the relief of me and my freshly soiled-up Depends. Let's see...big hat, big boots, ahhh...no fcuking cattle, you chinless face-forward prick. Y'all know what I'm talking about, right? That inbred face-forward-of-the-ears design. What a dick. I promptly ditched the weed, and an hour later waved through an impromptu drug check that Mr. Dork hastily set up on Hilton Head as if I would continue cruising around while holding that significant amount. Dumb shit. Empty. SLED drug dogs frantically sticking their Rover noses all around the seats, pondering whether or not to flappin' bark. Well, just FM. Big Stupid would demand indictment. What a dick. Many close calls. The lesson? It pays not to yap just to hear what it sounds like. Too bad I only now apply a shut mouth to matters of confidentiality and yap full steam ahead in freedom when most of that would be better better left unsaid to begin with.

It's a personal thing when there are certain agents involved, to my running the gauntlet. It invariably graduates from an investigation, though after a while, with such reliance upon pussy-boy snitches proving ineffective as such, the effort, through frustration, transforms into a hustle or even an obsession by drug enforcement. A street hustle whereby agents assume the intrigue, assume all the pretty women walking with gorillas down my street, and fat sacks of pleasure and defiance are included as automatic perks. They relish in the fake-ass defiance wherein they exhibit zero ability to run within the culture, which induces, to some degree, the world's normal people to "wish they were you." No one in history ever wished, "Gee, wouldn't it be cool if I could be another bottom-tier drug agent." Gimme a break. They don't know and will never know independence. Or freedom. As if those "hopelessly mired in mediocrity" types are suddenly and instantly knighted as hip by simply stepping into my illusion, so craved; once the true degree of insignificance is discovered on both sides, they wrestle profusely with their conscience to remain unrevealed with the only purpose being, of course, self-aggrandizement. Propping up their extremely misguided and misled role-playing efforts through the uselessness of total pricks lacking in every category. Lacking the minimum style, moxie, or gray matter to pull it off. Meant nothing to me back then. Carries over as less than nothing today. And tomorrow? A clean sweep.

In my heyday, my preference ride of choice was in turboprops with the company of pretty girls. Yeah, I mighta chased a couple women around, and yeah, all it got me was down. Down to Acapulco, down to Cancun, down to Cali—those type downs. Drug agent pricks didn't like that shit as they in contrast traveled elegantly in Crown Vics while stuffing their pie holes with Krispy Kreme bag-a-donuts and were relegated to the company of mostly fat ass women, not many of whom possessed those four critical knots. The pussy-boy snitches they recruited were usually better company and even a better class of losers most agents likely to recruit.

Chapter 27
Jury Trials, Military Brash, and Hawkins

OK, let's take a ride out West, shall we? There came a time for a reshuffle after my initial introductions to federal investigations, grand jury hearings, and then indictments. The federal indictments. Then came the federal drug trials, commonly referred to as Jackpot. I was another face in the first trial held in Charleston, South Carolina, by Federal Circuit Court Judge the Honorable Falcon Hawkins, presiding (Falcon Black Hawkins—imagine being tried by a person with that name! He was a fine jurist, though.) Well...I was acquitted by the jury of all charges during the course of that first trial in Charleston (83-165). Then promptly indicted in a parallel conspiracy a few weeks later (83-166), attending the second trial in Columbia with the same Judge Hawkins presiding. I was found guilty in that one, sentenced to ten years, and after appeal, checked into a minimum-security federal prison camp located in Montgomery, Alabama. Maxwell Air Force Base. Maxwell's silver hammer came down upon his head.

Remiss of me not to mention Federal Judge Hawkins, realizing my duty is to project some street-punk image when it comes to authority, especially when it comes to the ultimate figurehead, Judge Hawkins, representing the Feds, as was his position and sworn duty. After the many hours appearing before this man in charge, I must admit here that my mindset transitioned from the "local hoodlum element" to a true respect for this guy. He exhibited that demeanor not as an act but rather as the real McCoy. Stoic. Dignified. Being in his presence on a frequent basis, I'd stare at him during the many pretrial hearings. After a while something strange just began to come over me. It was a sense of guilt. That I was occupying this guy's space in my capacity as a nuisance and a complete waste of his time. If only such a man as Falcon Hawkins had been in my life prior, my ass likely wouldn't have been sitting there facing him in this ordeal to begin with. To compare him to my subsequent state judge, they were in totally different leagues. How to put this delicately...oh yeah. Lemme use that NFL versus Pop Warner analogy again. The big fish versus mullet one is appropriate as well. Total step and fetch, the state guy. Just a job, not a calling. Paging...any slug with a robe. That was Mr. State.

Sentenced to ten years, two five-year consecutives, by J. Hawkins. Served forty months. Flashed by in an instant. Moved back to Edisto and discovered just how boring it was here because all the drug smuggling nonsense had come to an abrupt end shortly before those two federal drug trials. At which point I moved my crusty ass to Hilton Head, South Carolina. Oh, my goodness. Man in the boat overboard. Now this was more like it. Opened a nightclub, a comedy club actually. And for the time being, for a couple years, it was a pretty safe gig. A fun life, making a few bucks, and coasting on the intrigue of all that I had been through previously, which, let me tell you what, was worlds away. A few faces from those heydays started hanging around, prodding me to get back in the game. Ultimately I put a couple of connections together, and when their worlds clashed and crumbled, all that baggage was directed back upon my stupid ass.

About this time the State of South Carolina was instituting a newly formed grand jury arm loosely modeled after the previously used federal strategy employed in the Jackpot investigations. The strategy relied more on the seizing of assets and the use of informants. There I was again in a two-year investigation, only this time as dictated by the whims of state agents, not the Feds. State agents lack the discipline of their federal counterparts. State agents all dream of one day being on the federal level. The Feds, however, employ far and away the higher standards, and many state agents, having applied to the federal system for employment, are relegated to work for state agencies having been determined not sharp enough or disciplined enough to cut the muster on the federal level. The bottom line is that state agents come at you in a far less organized manner. In all cases, in every pursuit of every defendant, no matter the jurisdiction, it is commonly known and just as commonly practiced that no matter the legality of the pursuit (i.e., concerning the rights of the would-be criminal targets), the second any defendant is arrested and subsequently pleads guilty, all prior acts under the actors and color-of-law participants are 100 percent forgiven. Period.

Through the state grand jury, I was indicted in a one-hundred-pound weed conspiracy facing twenty-five years mandatory . So I purchased an unlimited go anywhere travel ticket from Greyhound, and the next bus leaving was pointed out to me. Hopped my silly ass on that gus-bus and away we go. Couldn't help but notice a lot of heavier people ridin' those buses. Got me thinking about how I wasn't used to seeing larger people travel because I would mostly encounter the more healthy ones in Delta Rooms or chillin' out in first class at major airport hubs throughout the country. But what do ya know? Here the majority of carb eaters found. Ridin' on a bus. Someplace to go. Hey, me no ridicule or judge, OK? Not a hateful bone at play here...my preference is for slender women. May I have this preference? Grant me this leeway. For reasons already discussed. The understanding of poise and image is a biggie for me. Maybe to underscore my lack of it. Hey, you'll never hear me squawk regarding anyone's lifestyle, religion, choices, politics, nothing. It's your life, your decision and the preference thereof is squarely in your court. I may try to inform some people, to better relay info I truly believe has merit. Maybe some of it misplaced. Maybe some of it construed as arrogance. Not my intent at all. Your value of any info submitted is totally your call. Based entirely upon your parameters of worthiness.

OK. Back to the bus ride. First stop? Telluride, Colorado, then to San Fran Freako, eventually ending up in Reno, Nevada, busted there by South Carolina federal agents flying into Reno to attend a seminar or ski vacation. Thrown in a local jail awaiting South Carolina state extradition, then federal transport back to South Carolina jurisdiction. And it's at this point I wish to describe to you a couple of days amid the company of two US Marshals.

This is easy. Check this as real. They are badass. Physically imposing. Superbly well-spoken and trained. And they let you know quickly and up front that they ain't in the market to take any sorta bullshit. The two of them transported a gleesome threesome consisting of me, Charlie Rock, and Fifty Grand in a fed suburban from Reno, Nevada, to Sacramento, the capital of California. From there, we were off then to San Fran Freako, ending up at that city's airport. Now...at the end of a secluded runway at this airport, we witness the area completely surrounded by fully armed, locked-and-loaded federal big boys. Vans and LTDs and a 737 they called the CalgonJet, "'cause dat MF take you away, yo." All of us shackled souls were on our best behavior at this juncture.

Chapter 28
Heroes and Fed Readies

Jury trials. There are so precious few of them anymore unless defendants face beyond-absurd prison time and feel there is nothing to lose, so they exercise the right to a jury trial. The state's strategy is usually to make certain juries do not have the opportunity to hear all the circumstances of any crime. To hear the motivations from why anyone was indicted. To weigh the strategies for why some were indicted and others not. Juries are constantly instructed by judges to "judge only the facts," as if to say that even though you may not agree with the principles upon which these laws are based or the ethics apparent in the prosecution's conduct of the trial or punishment phase of the trial...you are compelled to rule only upon the evidence suggesting the charged crime was either committed or not. This is one method used by the courts in order to maintain their control over the proceedings, control that would surely be lost should juries be allowed to weigh all considerations. In drug trials the state attempts to cause members of juries to resent the defendant's easy life, smuggling drugs or gambling, speeding, or whatever (crimes against the dignity of the state) presumably identified.

This control is only made possible by "weed" the people relenting our power as members of any jury, and...this is why 98 percent of felony drug infractions involve guilty pleas as part of their resolution: we enable them through this individual power so granted to us. Not to them. To us. For us to be final judges on all aspects of criminal phases for which charges could be forthcoming.

Get nothing else from this read...get this.

Get the fact that all levels of bureaucrats fcuking love it that the general public considers jury duty a nuisance obligation almost everyone tries to avoid, that it's a pain in our ass to be summoned for jury duty, then have to report only to celebrate that we somehow lied and got out of it. And with this perception, we inadvertently cede the power of this most exclusive oversight so granted to "weed" the people over to said bureaucrats. For what? you may ask. For their ability to circumvent this associated power, which they convert into an aggregate monster powerful and unforgiving, allowing an easier path for control over a substantial period of time. Control of us. All of us.

What can we do about it? Consider jury duty your one shot left to inject sanity into government manipulation. You personally may right there and right now decide if you deem certain laws, procedures, punishments, and pursuits thereof reasonable. How? might you ask. You run something on a jury. Regardless of the charged offense, here's the rub.

In no manner of speaking am I suggesting we allow the bad guys unaccountable. Quite the opposite. But as you sit on any would be jury in any case before you...it's your shot to judge. Your shot to decide. Your shot to infuse reasonable judgement. This is not advice,OK? Its 100% information.

Now...the judge is gonna instruct you. Just so you know. It's called "charging" you. Judges tell you that you are only to decide the facts. Basically, that you're too stupid to concern yourself with other aspects in play here (i.e., admissibility, entrapment, punishment, sentence manipulation, and on and on it goes).

Take it from somebody who knows. During deliberations by a jury, jurors sometimes send the judge notes asking for clarity or whatever. About law. About punishment. They could ask, "If we find the defendant guilty, what's his likely jail time to serve? Give us his max. For the record."

Judges could and will answer, realizing the need to squash this line of questioning immediately: "The sentencing phase of this procedure is no concern of yours. You're only to discern the facts."

Well, here's one available response to that judge's answer that is an option for you.

"FokQ."

"Every aspect of this proceeding is my concern. Tell me now how much time—or at least a max time—a would-be found guilty defendant faces, or I will vote to acquit. And did I mention fokQ? Oh yeah. I forgot."

Simple. With this resolve, you take away the power of the court. The power to intimidate. The power to sell to a higher bidder. The power to trade for future favors. The very multibillion-dollar baby known as our legal system. It's not justice at all. It's about money and personalities involved in establishing clout. And stroke. Meanwhile, the broke defendant twists helplessly amid jacklegs, conditioned they are entitled to the very powers designed to prevent such situations.

Here's a quick example of the power jurors possess. You hear about all the cameras bureaucrats are installing everywhere with your money? To create more of an ongoing cash flow by writing us traffic citations sent to us in the mail? Here's one option we squash all that money-grab BS in its tracks. Demand a jury trial. Educated jurors could say, "We not gonna convict any citation issued via camera." And that kills that. Plain and simple. We have this power. These assholes only want your money. When you abandon your authority to keep your money, don't bitch when it's gone. Hello.

Two in one hundred defendants may actually seek a jury trial—pleading not guilty—usually having been so freaked out by threats of extreme punishments (exorbitant penalties) that they feel they "have nothing to lose" by doing so. Just about every son of a bitch you might know or have ever heard of getting arrested with significant or not-so-significant amounts of weed—or other drugs, for that matter—and receiving lighter punishments? Well...they rolled over on everything and everybody they knew, including your stupid ass. Don't fall for the story all snitches pass on to you, the explanations: "Oh, I had a good lawyer" or "It was my first time arrested." Yeah, they did have a good lawyer. The flappin' prosecutor is their attorney. Hello. Or another good one snitch boys like to throw around is in the area of "technicalities." A problem with a warrant or chain of custody, any of those. They all flip. They tell ya, "I did not ever testify against anyone." Most flips never actually testify because an actual jury trial almost never occurs. Most eventual flips have to be directed to shut the hell up. Enough already. Don't look now, but you are likely to fall into this category should some major shit ever hit your fan. Hey, man, nothing personal. The nature of everyday Square Ds. I simply go with the truth in the numbers. When you think about selling out, reconsider. I did, and all these years later, feel good, wouldn't change it. It felt good to say to the bought-and-paid-for pricks, "FokQ." I'm not saying anything. Get it like Drac, MF. And oh...one more thing, kiss my skinny, nonevolved monkey white ass." Not saying... just saying.

Once a guilty plea is agreed upon or entered into, any and all prior actions (defects) by the government (including law enforcement personnel) are 100 percent and forever nullified, absolved, or just gone. So don't fall for the bullshit, OK? People don't "get off." They roll their punk asses over, strap on wires, and do whatever it takes to spare their chickenshit little asses of prison or the mere inconvenience of it all. Remember this: snitches are thieves, cheaters, liars, and fokQ-groper pieces of shit. They are all one in the same. I'm not any of those, and my chickenshit ass was scared at the thought of prison big time too, but I got WTF over it. Chewed off major time. Over fifteen years. All I had to do was flip on the world and go back home to Mommy, where not too many would even have known my path. Could have lamented, "I had a good lawyer" or that the case had some "technical difficulties." All those drug-involved guys are propped up in most people's minds as daring or sharp enough to get away with it. Can you spell "rat bucket of shit"? "I had a good lawyer." Yeah, fokQ and your good lawyer, OK? Some of us know just what time it is and exactly just why that time matters.

Flip-boy pussy boys never talk about their involvement much except to like characters asserting their assumed authority. At the time snitch pricks justify their actions 'cause they want to "come clean." Wish to have a clear ride with society. All a crock of shit. The illusion of it all never stops. Probably 10 percent or less of these guys actually made weed smuggling possible. They were the guys in the trenches who could raise the money and sail the boats, had the balls to go to faraway places to procure the product. The rest of us rode our illusion in their wake. The snitch bitches, however, never talk about the "slinglin'," choosing instead to leave it to the imagination of the curious party craving some story of intrigue.

Not that there's a direct correlation here. Not even a thimbleful, but you know how many military guys don't like to speak of where they might have been deployed to? Well...in a not totally dissimilar manner, many military guys choose to keep quiet about details due to the fact they're better off riding that wave of illusion as well, the wave of honor and badassery a mere 10 percent of military in real terms, actually possesses and exudes. Not everybody is amazing, you know? Or is a hero. BTW, uDam has visited Arlington National Cemetery. I get it.

Here's a quote by a guy named Michael Yon. A real military man: "Everyone wants to be a hero until they have to do hero shit." So true. Then what?

Most everyday guys confronted with combat conditions find out very quickly they simply aren't equipped to deal with it like it was hoped or expected they might be. Despite the training. Despite the investment. My numbers reveal to me also, that I likely would fall into this category.

But to those 10 to 15 percent of you military guys? The grit rippers? You are the reasons dweebs such as me may ramble as we please. You few, you proud, a lot of times feel not the need to relive that elevated level of grit you're able to. For you wish not to stand out, demeaning the lesser contributions from supporting personnel. So please don't assume pure audacity in my daring to seemingly begrudge those sorts defining our military. Not so. As in the rest of society, there are precious few living up to the hype reserved for the rugged and the real MFs. You guys know the rub but choose not to denigrate the other 90 percent tagalongs. Hey somebodys gotta work the mess halls, fuel the hardware, maintain security, mow the freakin'grass. All heros? No. So why discuss it? I've a boatload of empathy to ALL military personnel, recognizing you all are placed at risk due to our country's perpetual missions involving massive amounts of created money, borrowed money, subsidizing this senseless outlay. No fault of any of our military personnel. And as a country we must and shall fulfill our promises to ALL military members. Period. My intent here is strickly to break down the numbers while recognizing and saluting the exceptional 10-15 percent actually carrying the torch.

Again, you ten percenters represent the might and limitless majesty through the mere threat of the US Military. Thus, the sole reason weed the people afforded the right whereby submitting a tritely bullshit essay of thoughts from a local hoodlum becomes the ultimate privilege. So to you select guys in the military, in fire departments, on the police force, in all law enforcement agencies, to that one gal at every prison in the front office that runs the entire place...to all you ten-percenters...hats off to you all in a big way. I get it.   And propose a toast:

"Long answered ever questions sleep spare truth some drink dimmed fool,
A glass may toast twin Eagles deep we raise whose strength must rule."
–Salute

Chapter 29
Can't Seize This

Lets imagine you're the state and you take the position pricks like me are indifferent to the state's dignity and therefore deserving of pursuit and indictment. And also, according to certain of those in charge, persons like me are deserving of extended prison time—why? Because I'm directly responsible for the real crimes committed by true criminals in order street criminals may gather the funds necessary to purchase said weed which I personally smuggled in and offer for sale. That it's on me and 'this local hoodlum element needs to be shut down.' As if street crime would then cease or at least recede. Total BS. They know this particular explanation to be a crock. After all, LEOs can't very well proclaim their actual objectives in investigating me are as follows:

There is zero risk to law enforcement in pursuit of nonviolent types;

I'm more likely to possess assets they may seize and enjoy as their own;

By being white, relieves the notion most drug arrests target black men;

And when uDam should flip to snitch-bitch, the pot just got sweetened.

So, they may now proclaim instead, it's imperative the state devote available and valuable resources as to "eliminate one of the primary incentives driving street crime in society overall."

Here's a question for ya. About that 'because criminals commit real crimes to acquire monies to purchase weed from me' thing? Hey. Why wouldn't street guys just rob us instead? I'm right over here, hiding behind that stack of weed in the open. Easy peasy. Smugglers were pursued simply due to law enforcement's assumed notion we had some slick shit they wanted to seize for themselves. Has nothing to do with real criminals committing petty shit sandwich crimes to buy weed. Most of them sling weed to begin with. However, and here's the biggie, most of them are broke asses. LEOs are sick of 'em all. Lower tier street druggies are mainly just low tier druggie types and typically broke. Not to mention, their unrelenting decades long being the absolute nuisance to Law enforcement they are. It wears both on society and LEOs after a while. And the weed we smuggled is somehow responsible for this? Gimme a break. Hell, I'd much prefer the organized pursuit of me also. Any day. A much better story, instead the one about some broke ass holding a Glock in my face.

Aren't we all pleased that true criminals do not rob people and then use the stolen money to, say, pay their property taxes? Would it then be a former property tax bureaucrat writing a book about being locked up, for said bureaucrat was blamed as the cause of the crime itself based simply upon mere conjecture as to what the actual criminally obtained money was subsequently spent on? Imagine that. Stupid as hell. Well, it wasn't ridiculous for any of those duck billed pricks seeking a justified pursuit of my nowhere ass. Crime is about character...or lack thereof...just as mercy and demeanor are surely a part of our DNA under the caption of "civility." Sure, I broke the law. So what? I jaywalked too. But didn't receive twenty-five years mandatory for jaywalking. Whose laws are these? Who decides twenty-five years for a weed conspiracy is pragmatic—is logical—while stolen billions from public coffers are punishable by bailouts, fraud, and zero time in prison? Come to think of it, who has benefited from the tens of millions of people being arrested for weed infractions? Why is it that in practically every town in this country, one may score an endless variety of dope on a given street corner? And do you, the people—who sit on the ever-diminishing number of trials before an actual jury—agree with the drug laws, their effectiveness, or the manner in which they are administered? The punishment? Where are the victims tumbling about in the wake of my hoodlum's escapade? So excuse me while I vent, and question authority and sensibility. And have a little fun and hopefully spare some younger person a boatload of grief, but for the mere lack of ever-so-protected information. And while we're at it, enough of the weed shit too. Seriously. You're stupid enough without it. Bank that one too.

My "crime" was indignity toward the state. My real "crime"—as it was—was refusing to strap on undercover wires and go to work for our state's law enforcement division (SLED). This is why I chewed off 4,477 days in real prisons for noncooperation. The weed was nothing more than the gateway perpetuating the hustle of law enforcement in order they personally may seize assets from those such as I that might have a little something to grab. A pursuit motivated by statutes permitting actual ownership of "drug-related" property seized, usually pursuant to some snitch bitch swearing said assets resulted from illicit gains. After all, it's the very nature of government to possess that which they cannot produce, for if they were so capable, they wouldn't be in government to begin with. Simple enough.

Stirring up the dumb masses is easy when all that is required is to focus on the shit the dumb masses don't possess, pointing to druggies who have "everything" and seemingly mocking the little people amid their everyday struggles. Agents default to offended mode when they perceive another as having it easy or perceive another as born richer, smarter, or better-looking than them. The main such dololly Square D slug against me was some such clown about town. The only significance this jack-off ever dreamed was just that, in his own head, pertaining to the "local hoodlum element" such as myself. He saw me publicly as some hoodlum punk poisoning the world when really he defaults to the assumption I could contribute towards his meal ticket to notoriety and all the free shit he'd house once he flipped me over to "his bitch" status. He had the power. Had me locked up for over a decade. His call. My regret. Pursued me with hundreds of thousands in state money for a couple years prior, betting I would flip soft and become his little bitch like his number-one little bitch (where right here I was tempted to identify him, but what the hell. I got over it). Bottom line, I did not bitch up or strap up. Meant nothing then, means nothing now, and it ain't gonna mean jack shit tomorrow either...except that is to me—that is of course, *except* to me.

These type renegade LEOs create crime every day. It's called sentence manipulation, and the legal accountability of said practices is all forgiven once the flip bitch pleads guilty (as they mostly all do. Mostly here equaling about 99%). And in many instances the guilty plea much easier to procure once these various enhancements presented as all the more reason for defendants to flip. A common and more easily understood example of the many sentence manipulations commonly invoked by LEOs might involve a drug agent following around a suspected drug courier. Whereby the suspect is almost always apprehended once they happen to drive by a school zone, for there is a proximity enhancement of five years should a defendant be busted with dope near any school. Has zero to do with the suspect slinging sacks of weed through the chain link fence to fourth graders, as the law is intended to curtail. Agents of the law simply wait until the suspect drives near any school, then moves in. Simple enough. This practice may only be challenged during an actual trial. Pretty much. Cannot be challenged in any manner upon entering the plea of guilt. Remember this when you're driving around pulling on a blunt. Avoid school yards. Hello. Or if you must partake, just go home and light that fire. Stupid ass.

All my poor little face-forward shit prick agent achieved on behalf of the state for his efforts and the hundreds of thousands of state dollars he wasted? Was my broke ass. He simply moved on to the next more predictable breaker of laws.

Most drug special agents simply cannot process the fact that I possess one thing they can never seize.

Please read that one again...They have no fucking clue that I possess something their dolt asses will never know and cannot ever seize. Something completely foreign to them and void amid their empty Square D boring ass world. One cannot very well seize something they lack the capacity to even identify, much less take. Still don't. So fuck them. Another visit to an exotic beach somewhere for a little volleyball could be on the table. Stupid asses will never know my moments. The society. The Ms. Joanster. The Society. This passion for life and liberty. Seize this, MF. A mere void from a mere Square D; replaceable and forgotten in three minutes flat. Having actually promoted drug exploitation rather than having subdued it. All day, everyday.

Chapter 30
Last First Date

OK. What a release that was. When I released from prison the second time as the two-time big dumb-ass loser, I was on a first date with my last gal, my best gal, and my current gal. It was the same gal, and she still is. We had tickets to attend a chamber music concert at the Presbyterian Church on Edisto Island. Hey, there were some nerves there, for sure. She already made it clear that she was quite puzzled about going out with a convict. With a convict wearing an ankle bracelet, no less. With a convicted drug smuggler, she previously announced publicly that she had never once done drugs, never wanted to do drugs, and never even seen any drugs. Making it perfectly clear that any and all illicit drug activity of any sort was simply off the table, as in off her table. In addition, and this was a biggie for a yapper like me, she was not the least bit interested in any of the BS stories either. Despite those pronouncements and, yes, sporting the WTF look on her face as we entered the church, we did so not as mere somebodies showing up but rather as an arrival. We already reviewed where that one comes from. One may plan to show up. But to arrive? It requires that *it* factor. *It* people are aware of it.

We were greeted by an elder of the church. A wonderful man I'd known for decades. Rock-solid guy. David Lybrand. Not that it's my prerogative to mention many real people in here, though in this exceptional case, I hope I am not out of line. He was a fabulous teacher to me, as my observing his example. Could have used more of it. He had no idea about my wasted efforts on the many dead-end avenues, but the man shook my hand that evening, recognizing the turn had indeed taken place.

Then he said, "Welcome back, Skippy. You're in for some awesome music; follow me, and I'll seat y'all at your family's pew."

My soon-to-be best gal said, "Wow, your family has a pew here?" I said looks like it, and there we sat. You ever wanted to jump around and holler out complete with street edge, "Dat's right. We got a family pew! I'm somebody. Who let the dawgs out? Who the baby daddy? Somebody call Oprah." But alas, I backed off the temptation. Paid my respects on a couple of folded knees before God in his house as honoring our Creator. A few minutes later, my date asks, "Is that marble plaque on the wall there in homage to someone from your family? Is that why this is the family pew?" I said I didn't really know about that, but the plaque had the name of none other than my great-great-(maybe another great)-grandfather.

Hey, what can I tell you? She was impressed. So was I. Funny how things shake out and the joy inside me for the first time in fifty-four years. I had grown up there and was proud to be there, grateful to be free, and humbled to be welcomed.

Which got me thinking about that significance—about the man whose legacy was in part represented by a plaque etched out on a small church's wall. And I couldn't help but wonder as well how that man on the wall might regard me at this point in my life. All I could do was regard him. Wonder about his journey to this place. How did he get a plaque on the wall? Was it a gesture of sincerity, or did he throw down a chunk for the accolade? Was he real, or was he merely wealthy? Were they powerful men back then, large and in charge, rendering the community simply too afraid to confront them or question their actions or their demeanor? Were they thriving amid some forgiving masquerade? Or were they genuine and good-natured? Did they donate a church to absolve themselves of any misgivings? To bolster and acknowledge the vital contributions of the wifey? Or was he back then sincere and flushed up to the point that substantial donations didn't mean much in the larger picture and plaques were cheap? Hell, I don't know, for I did not know him. Could merely hope they were genuine souls and everything they appeared or were remembered to be. My parents and grandparents placed a lot of faith in the nobility of such deceased souls in raising us, emphasizing the importance, prestige, and value of goodness and virtue, based upon their assumed goodness indeed. The importance of genealogy and history, along with our duty to honor the meaning therein. I guess to impress us with the notion that perhaps we are indeed special through these precious virtues being passed along and that we as participating subjects should conduct ourselves in a manner of gratitude and resolve. It is a rather tough act to follow if actual and a rather tedious one to emulate should we lack the ability to represent ourselves in such the proper manner and style.

Wow. The best date ever. We drove to Charleston after the concert as I'd requested and received permission to bust my nine o'clock curfew. Thanks to my federal probation officer, Tammy, and thanks to my dear friend Preppie for guiding me through the forgotten perils of the dating scene and five-star restaurants when finding myself out of the loop for over a decade. What a life, people. Wake up and live it.

Chapter 31
A Solitary Man

My spending months and months in solitary confinement came as a shock, adding to this story's dismay. Here's a large part of what rendered solitary tolerable. It was songs. All guys in solitary reside in eight-by-eight cells. Comfy enough. A little cold all the time, though it could have been much, much worse. Most guys participated in songs, especially at night and on weekends mostly. TGIF, baby. Applied in there too. The ways guys would communicate and pass contraband around was really clever. A guy staying on the second floor above me one day ordered me to "flush your toilet on the count of three." Since I didn't have a whole lot going on, I said, "Sure thing." Three, two, one. Bam. A wrapped-up small package appeared in my toilet. Then he instructed me to pass it along to the cell next door. Which happened. A few minutes later, I got a good whiff of some fine Colombian. Right interesting. So were the top songs in solitary. Here they are:

#5 "Brick House"
#4 "I Feel Good"

#3 "Me and Mrs. Jones"
#2 "I Can Feel It Coming in the Air Tonight"
#1 "Roxanne"

Oh, the memories of being in solitary. It was used as a tool of coercion, trying to get me to rat boy regarding the smuggling of cell phones. Fcuk them. I didn't rat any of the guards either. One time a prison admin prick proposed a plea deal (strictly as to absolve prior defects by the agency) and I asked, "Could you let me ponder on it and I call ya on a cell later?" these guys have zero sense of humor.

So they locked my ass up. There are very strict policies regarding using solitary for such purposes. Keeping people locked down until they cooperate. The guidelines require that if an inmate be held for more than twenty-four hours in solitary with no charges, the warden must sign off on it. They didn't charge me with anything. Just had some snitch bitch rat me because I wouldn't allow his broke ass to use a cell phone as he was in a jam having been busted with strips (small amounts of weed, five bucks each). No matter. Course he instantly gives me up. The nature of rats as 95% of the world are. Further on regarding solitary, to hold inmates in solitary for up to seventy-two hours with no charges requires a regional prison director's sign off. The next step, whereby an inmate is held without charges for a week or so, requires that the state director of prisons be notified and sign off on the continued misuse of solitary confinement.

Those buckets of shit held me for 107 days with zero charges. The main objective? As mentioned prior, whenever those in authority, under color of law, solicit any guilty plea from the subject, all prior illegal acts by those in charge are 100 percent voided. They simply vanish. As such, toward the end of my 107-day illegal solitary stay, they went so far as to offer a plea bargain to the very minimal charge of "out-of-place." By doing so, this action would have exonerated these shitbags. So instead, I delivered 'em a festive fuck you. They were pissed. Had the power. I was transferred to another prison that night. Upon arrival there the next day, yet another bucket of shit in a seemingly endless procession of idiocy was instructed to charge me with attempted escape, which he did, in the process saving his fellow SCDC hacks back in solitary oversight at the previous shithole. I was tossed back into solitary for another several months. The first eight days of which spent in a suicide watch cell. All for the purpose of coercion. Another 167 days to follow. The charge of "escape"? I prevailed, and that charge was reversed through the course of due process. Grateful for it.

Then I sued the department for the many illegal uses of solitary. I was very pissed off, and the only recourse was to sue the sorry shits. And who'd a-guessed? Lost that one on a fabricated technicality, for just another fat ass appointed circuit judge ruled my filing "untimely." Ruled that such filings are allowed one year to facilitate. Judge Fat Ass Sorry Prick ruled that my one-year deadline to file suit began the moment the defect of misused solitary policy actually occurs, when the defect was, or should have been, first known. Not when the complaint adjudicated as case law seemed to infer. Therefore, roughly 270 days of that one-year period of restraint continued to lapse while my chilled ass remained in solitary. That one-year period should have tolled until such time as the "attempted escape" totally fabricated bullshit charge failed the agency and the state's argument during my due process presentation. There's another fresh load of dignity for ya. Fuck them. Don't wish to dwell on this much more, for usually an inmate's plight over unfair treatment and charges pretty much maxes out the outer limits of one's tolerance of "boring." Just don't have cell phones in your cell. Wouldn't have been any solitary. Hell, I thought that's why they call 'em cell phones. FM.

Many higher up administrative positions in South Carolina prisons? Filled by employees who—well, let's put it this way—could have worked on the federal level. They earn really good money, can't be bought, and are very capable to process the never ending whims of thousands of men with nothing better to do than to bitch. Nonstop. I'm talkin' firsthand the observing of captains, associate wardens, and especially the big dawg wardens themselves. Hey, they in charge of keeping my silly ass safe during incarceration. And I thank y'all for that. Had nothing to do as to why I was there either. Didn't matter. My ass got through it all in tact with a lot of dependency from the actual ones large, in charge, and thank goodness for us all... running something.

Now the lower tier prison officials are not quite the same story. Again, there was a means for me to avoid solitary and the exposure to lower tier prison guards. Don't smuggle in cell phones.

Many guys come up and say to me, "Hey, I never ratted either. Guess me a real tough guy too." However, the numbers suggest otherwise to me. Welcome to the brotherhood. Well, maybe you never had the option to rat. Maybe you were sharp enough to allow only me to be your go-between on that fine line of badge, edge, balance, excitement, and a few bucks. Good choice. You owe me nothing. To you COs that brought me items in prisons, you owe me nothing. For it was I alone who decided your crime, your culpability, your guilt, and your punishment. Hey, as previously stated, I'm not tough guy alright? Not even close. Flashback baby, to having received a get-out-of-jail free card one night in a nondescript Beaufort driveway, I'm reminded to pass along some of that same compassion to some, where appropriate, both to some locked up and to some remaining free. I deemed you not guilty. You owe me zip.

uDam Skippy's dignity is not only free; it's also genuine. Whereas the state's dignity is nothing more than a prop usually exercised for the assumed benefit of some state slug. And hey, I felt their power. And it felt very empowering, lemme tell you. Imagine such absolute power with zero consequences. Mind-blowing. I never spared anybody (spared = not snitch) for fear of retribution but rather having judged they would be targets, undeserving of the actual extent to which the state's so-called "dignity" was able and or likely to extort them. And you know what? Well, I never been to Spain either. And WTF does that have to do with it? Exactly.

There is a book memory most vivid from the suicide watch cell within a solitary confinement cell block known as Jasper Unit SMU (special management unit) located at a maximum-security state facility in Allendale, South Carolina. A real dive. The book was the only reading material I was allowed to possess at that time. Not a paperback writer, mind you. For those eight days, it was just me and that book. That's it. No clothes to speak of (except when I could bribe "runarounds" to steal and deliver me some articles of clothing—oh, the term "runaround" refers to trustee-type inmates assigned to bring food and otherwise cater to the endless whims of solitary guys). So a paper blanket and a stupid-ass look on my face—these items defined my stint in solitary. At the risk of running everyone off...the one book I am referring to is the Bible. Still have that very same one. Going into 283 days of solitary was my coming out, and during those special suicide-watch eight days, I vowed to write my own book one day.

First of all let me say this about all this non-ratting, snitching, dewboy bitching—whatever tag we put on it—that it is, in my opinion, not any sort of heroic action. It is merely a personal decision. The few men and women I knew, as did I myself also, based this decision on a longer-term reflection of character and life in general. Granted, what we were involved in was illegal. So I wish not to glamorize any part of stupid decisions even when some reach out and comment on how brave it was and how much guts it took not to give up the world. In fact, a better connection shared in today's time is how an average guy having an average life and likes to hunt and fish with his children. Mine was another one of those decisions that simply is what it is, which precluded me from ever enjoying those times gone by watching my kid catch his first fish or hit his first home run. Don't go all boo-hooing now. I already got that one covered. However, it was a mindset. A chosen one, albeit a rather selfish one, no less. As previously described, it was indeed the quality DNA rushing through some still, nonetheless, chickenshit veins. I'd been raised to be true to my word and remember fondly the process, this notable virtue transitioned from thought to mindset. Again, don't go and etch the GD trophy either. I am no tough guy. In my experiences people who tend to brag about money are typically broke, while guys who brag about all the women are typically single and sloppy slugs and couldn't get laid in a woman's prison with a fistful of pardons. Therefore, when some tend to brag about how they were not snitch boys, it leads me to believe they would've been at the drop of a hat or that dime had they ever been faced with the fear of such an imposition. Under pressure (crank that one up). Had they ever been indicted by a grand jury with the express purpose of the expectation they gonna roll? No. Had they ever been arrested and faced a decade or two in a penitentiary, but prior to being hauled off, they were offered one opportunity to sit in an interrogation room at the Charleston Custom House (and no, that's not a high-end restaurant either). Being interrogated by a very determined and uniquely trained federal agent and commanded that they should think very carefully about the next answer for it may very well determine their fate for the next couple decades? Negative. I remember such events vividly as every law enforcement division's primary objective is to extract from a defendant first their cooperation, through the coveted guilty plea. I say people. *What?* I've heard all those hard-luck tales from all of you U.S. males. Spare me the rest of the story, please. Too boring. Too fake. Put it in your book.

This is precisely what the numbers reveal. If you allow them the platform to reveal. What's new? Not a personal thing, mind you. Numbers are key. They can size you up and break you down. If you're not a numbers person, you likely stand your fat ass in lines to buy lottery tickets. 'Cause you don't know the numbers. You only know the intrigue and impulse of the here and now. It's fun. Somebody's gotta win. The lottery in South Carolina came to exist in 2002 because state actors envied private people making bank on video poker. The numbers for the more recent lottery years, BTW, in South Carolina roughly shake down pretty much as follows:

Let's use the figure of $2 billion per year in lottery revenue (much more than that, actually). Half of this fleece goes toward reeling the dumb masses into continuing to play (as is the primary objective of every casino). Thirty percent goes toward the education fund, which is the advertised purpose of the scam (as if any of state actors give a rip about that one). "But wait!" he cries. The real motivation for the scam, and it's a royal one at that, it's called the "administration fee." Twenty percent! And since we're all numbers people now...how much is 20 percent of $2 billion? Yeah right! Most of you right now wouldn't have the first edge of an idea. And you're exactly where the state needs you to be. Buying tickets. Fat and stupid clinging to a soda and sacks of Doritos, holding up the lines at convenience stores. Deer and headlights. And exactly why is the state allowed to be a bookie and a casino? "It's all about the children's education." Horseshit.

As a matter of fact in many bureaucratic settings, a main objective of working under the umbrella of "for the people" is certainly not the state's employee's salary either, much less any imagined, much less a profound purpose. More times than not, what draws people to working for and working as a bureaucrat are the powers and perks that come with it. The fact remains that it is extremely difficult to be fired from any state position. One offering a pretty good health care plan, and the potential for an even better retirement plan. A retired bureaucrat's monthly check is usually based somewhat on his or her highest salary for a period of several years during the course of, though usually towards the end of, their esteemed career run. It's an unwritten rule that when many government workers come near retirement, other government workers strive in unison to elevate that pivotal period, so the calculating formula is indeed the highest retirement amount possible. And some, perhaps quite a few such instantly replaceable Square D types are afforded positions with the lottery commission on their way out the door that add to this higher basis for monthly retirement checks, the outlay of which we, the endearing public shall be straddled with for decades. Everyone in gov.me facilitates such strategies for moving on out later on, naturally expecting the same considerations upon their own curtain call one day down the line. And there you have a good chunk of the 20 percent administrative fee within the lottery commission. Not only does it insure future monies for 'em, but in many cases, it is used as a tool, as an outlet, a portal, if you will, to get rid of the more useless or needful ones and to boost retirement amounts as a "thanks" for the sterling Square D performances. And PS, we're all happy to see you go along with the nonstop boring ass pictures of crack baby grandchildren and yapping shit machine little dogs, too, shittin' up every weekend barbecuer's yard. Here's your watch. Time to ride out. Just leave the state's fake ass dignity at the gate, OK?

And what's killing many Northern states is that when their slaves retire and they begin to draw these exorbitant monthly checks, the retiree then decides to move south. Killing all hope that their home state will ever reap any benefit from the monthly dollars being issued. That's why a lot of those states bask in red ink, never to recover unless propped up by printed federal reserve money.

Chapter 32
What Are Your Lottery Odds Anyway?

On the lam. During the course of my illustrious drug career, I went on the lam twice. The first time was in the eighties, when I heard about the federal grand jury in session looking into the beginning phases of what came to be known as the Jackpot trials. Started hearing my name come up in some of this secretive grand jury testimony, and it was then deciding to carry my ass out West. This first time on the lam was a breeze, for at the time, I was neither wanted nor indicted. I ended up going to Del Mar, California, and for these few months, it was the closest I ever came to a pampered life as a young, fairly rich, healthy guy. One day I got bored and bought a sweet little 1971 280 SL in a showroom window at the behest of a cutie pie young waitron longing for the West Coast Hiway breezes in her hair. Chocolate brown with a light brown interior, think it was twenty-five grand. People in California were quick to take cash, as opposed to people in South Carolina, who seemed to be deathly afraid of anything over the amount of three hundred dollars in twenties. Next came a trick crib on the beaches built on a cliff overlooking the Pacific (the Atlantic is the one over here). It was a grand time. And the thought was, the gauntlet was closing in; why not cull through a couple hundred large in very short order? Kinda stupid, yeah, but this is what kinda stupid, yeah, dumb asses do with easy money. Alas, one becomes bored of dreary old West Coast living as boredom sets in, and back to good old South Cackalacky it was. Got indicted and went to the first trial of the Jackpot ordeal, and, as already discussed, acquitted. Kinda shocking to me to buy a couple of the stupid ass snitches off in the parking lot across from 82 Queen in Charleston. It was sorta ironic, in a way, meeting for the first time one of the snitches scheduled to testify against me the next day. Just called him up at his hotel and said, "Hey, man, let's meet and greet for a beer." And he shows up at the Queen about twenty minutes later.

That was the nature of the organization at the time, where a guy, having been fully debriefed about me and having signed the deal to testify and, in fact, planning to testify the next day, had zero hesitation to meet the stranger he was snitching on the night before, for a beer. Such gentlemen. Didn't know the guy very well and wasn't even introduced to him until the day before, when, hell's bells, my lawyer and I went to talk to the guy.

So we were in the parking garage, sitting in Rocket—a very tricked out 930 Porsche Turbo. Lotta fricking good it was doing me about now. But anyway, the guy went on about how he felt like the government was screwing him and he was very displeased with his treatment. Just goes to show you that once you plead guilty, the prosecutors see you as totally expendable. Don't much give a shit about you before you plead guilty and even less afterwards. We sucked back a couple chatty cocaine for the membrane lines, and when asked whether he would be interested in misidentifying me during his testimony the next day, he responded, "Well, I sort of signed a deal where it's required the truth be said." At this point he was offered some real truth. A chunk of Benjies totaling 'bout fifteen large (ahhh, that would be 150 bills).

"That true enough for ya?"

He said he liked my truth better, and with that he hopped out of the time machine and said, "You take it easy, Richard."

Sure enough, the next day at trial, he was up there doing what little bitch-ass snitches do with one of his good lawyers (like, attorneys all snitches have, you know). The prosecution said, "OK, do you recognize the defendant Skippy Sanders in this courtroom today?"

And the guy said, "Yes, I do."

"Would you be so kind as to point this gentleman out?"

"Yes, that's him sitting right over there," he said as he pointed his finger at some other dweeb sitting there looking all stupid. And that was that. A few days later, the jury deliberated and came back with a not-guilty verdict. A couple of the jury members sat with me soon after back at 82 Queen sipping nectar, and they told me the number-one reason for my acquittal was not the misidentification. There were many of those. All day, everyday.

Rather, it was that we demonstrated how the government was constantly using the family off-load site also. And the former jurors lamented that they considered such action facilitating exactly the charges the trial was about didn't seem just. But aside from that, they wanted to know if I was in fact guilty or not. "Yes. Guilty, but only of providing an off-load spot, not of the entire indictment conspiracy as charged." Cheers. The glove did not fit. Had to acquit.

But no matter. After the acquittal, the lead prosecutor indicted me again a few days later on a "parallel conspiracy," which normally would require that the government show a separate and distinct agreement, which they didn't, for there wasn't one. It was 100 percent double jeopardy, but no one gives a shit, not then, not now, or not ever. My conspiracy was established with Flash to use the off-load site. From then on, Flash used the site exclusively. Then one fine day he sold the off-load spot and directed another group to come offload some payload there. My original agreement with him remained untarnished but doesn't matter. Found guilty this time around. And that's about it. Kinda boring and really and not even worth writing about. Ole Falcon Hawkins handed me ten years, and I chewed off forty months at Maxwell Air Force Base in Montgomery, Alabama. It's one of the best places in the world to do time; at least it was at that time until the crackhead brigade took over and spoiled yet another pristine neighborhood.

Chapter 33
Choppin' It Up on the Lam

The next lam chop comes amid the roaring nineties, the Milli Vanillies. Hell, they were fake asses; I might as well be too. They couldn't sing, and I didn't sing. Same MO for LEOs, except this time it was in state court implementing a newly formed state grand jury drug task force model after the federal drug task force under which the Jackpot trials came to be. You could say I was a floundering father of that effort. (Floundering father! Cool!) It was a three-year process, and I was indicted, facing a twenty-five-year mandatory sentence, and it came time for trial, and I said fokQ, hopped my ass on a Greyhound, and headed west. Only this time... was wanted, flat broke with no destination and no identification. First stop? San Fran Freako, where it was quite expensive to live. So hopped on a gambling shuttle and ended up in Reno, where I was dumped off in front of the Circus Circus Hotel and Casino. Waltzed my ass in there and asked how much for a room, and they said six hundred bucks. Gimme another big fat FM, please. Ended up at some dump renting a room by the week. For the next couple of weeks, tried to figure out how to come up with an identification. A driver's license. Figured out a pretty good system by finding a recently deceased man my age whose circumstances fit three specific criteria. And back in 1995, it was possible and rather easy to do this. Today, establishing a fake ID that is police compatible is simply not happening, so the three criteria may be revealed: the person had to have been born in one state, lived in another state, and become deceased in a third state. It was about that easy. The first time at the Reno DMV office with my stack of papers explaining my recent 'move' there and my wish to transfer my license... oh shit. The guy's death certificate was poking out in the stack of papers sitting on the DMV lady's desk. Grabbed the stack and plucked the cotton-picking death certificate from among the papers. Thank you very much.

Now. For the first time in my life, I had to go and apply for a job. The first place applied to was a spot out there in Reno, a workout center looking for someone to chase down the workout center contractual agreements that had been breached. Wasn't very good at that job. One day the receptionist there said there was this lady on the phone saying that she was moving to Reno, and her brother told her to look me up to show her around and help her find a suitable apartment. My response? "I'll come out of the building right now with my hands over my head." Very paranoid. Turns out her brother and the deceased person whose name had now been assumed by me were buddies while in college back at UNLV. My fake name was Richard E. Smith. And she was able to look me up because of the public phone book listing trying to pose as a normal everyday slug. This lady was quite persistent, and we set up a meeting at the Peppermill Casino after work. We met at the Peppermill, and she went on all about her brother while she was assuming the whole time that her brother and me were quite the item back then, and it began to dawn on me that we could have been butt buddies? Whaaaaat? Or something? It was quite a blow.

"Oh, Richard, you don't have to pretend. My brother told me so much about you, and he said you'd be the perfect tour guide for this fair city and could show a gal where she might prefer to live as opposed to the side of town she might want to avoid." And for a couple of days, after work, we drove around and learned the landscape of the town together. It was about this time that, over an adult beverage at one of the casinos, she said to me, "Excuse me Richard if I'm out of line, but frankly, you don't strike me as a gay man."

At that point came some mild little rant about how people try certain things in college and sorta get over it. "I'm not gay anymore; decided to leave my friends behind; wasn't all it was cracked up to be, got tired of coming home shit faced." Stop it already! Sammy's jokes anyway.

When she wanted to call her brother one day and have us talk…well, that simply could not happen. Told her that we've both moved on. Could then foresee this was headed for a not-so-happy conclusion one day where the brother would just pop up in town and see me and probably tell this girl that something sure was kind of fishy here. So had to tell this charming, very sharp young gal in a strange city seeking out a bit of security and trying to be careful that "maybe we better not continue to enjoy one another's company starting now." The poor lady almost cried, and as for me? Have you ever seen a squonk's tears? Well look at mine. Just look at mine. What on earth was I doing here. Not a top ten moment. Pass me the hanky.

Had to leave that job at the workout center for I couldn't risk the sister snooping around. My next job was at Advantage Rent a Car. The nice people there treated me like a normal Joe. Exactly what I wanted. Told the manager that my preference wasn't to work at the airport because of an ex-fiancée who worked at another rental car agency and that we had agreed to live separate lives, which included not working in the same area. My manager fully understood this and assigned me to a small satellite operation located in Incline Village, near Lake Tahoe, at a car dealership where cars were rented mostly to people dropping off their cars to be worked on.

One day, out of the blue, my manager asked, "Hey, Richard, I'm sorta in a jam and would like to ask you a favor, realizing your situation with the ex-fiancée. When does she work at the other car rental desk?" All these words still ring so true to me to this day. Not knowing what to say or where this was leading, my response was that she pretty much worked weekdays from nine to five. My manager said, "Oh, this is great." It was a Sunday night in April (Tiger had just won his first master's). The manager went on to explain that the girl working the desk at Advantage was having a surprise anniversary party thrown for her, and they needed someone to fill in for her the last two hours she was scheduled to work that Sunday night. Couldn't say no. "Sure, I'll be happy to fill in for her." Some strange shit went down in those couple hours.

One of my first people at the counter that evening was this man wishing to rent a car, and as I was doing some paperwork, he told me he did not have a credit card. "Hey, no credit card, no car."

He said, "Come on, man, I really need to get to my kids. I'm very worried about them for their drunk-ass mommy refuses to let me talk to them. Something really bad could be happening. You just gotta make an exception; let me rent this car. Here's the cash, and I can also put down a sizable deposit."

At this point I just told the guy, "It's not happening; you gotta move on."

He tried other rental agencies, and about forty minutes later, he came back to me and said, "You are the only hope. No one else will even talk to me about it.

"OK, man, I can't get your car, but you could borrow my roommate's car, which is being used to get me to work. It's a piece of junk; it belongs to my roommate, and you give me two grand down, and you can take it. " He said he only had $1,000. "OK. How 'bout this? When my shift is over, I'll just drive you where you need to go. Take it or leave it."

He said, "Thanks so much. Will wait till you get off work, and off we will go. Really do appreciate it."

The evening at the Reno Airport Advantage Rent-a-Car counter is winding down. My last renters are standing at the counter as their statement is being prepared. Contract, all that, and instructions as to how to get to their car. The rental car counters at this airport are set up in a long row like most of them are. At the end of this long row was a door to the left where employees would exit the building at the end of their shifts. Beyond those doors were seventy-five yards or so of various taxi and shuttle services, many of which offered rides to various casinos in town and to the resort towns of Lake Tahoe and Incline Village. The shuttle area was filled with throngs of newly arrived jetsetters chomping at the bit to get on the ski slopes. Wouldn't you know that the two ladies waiting on their last rental for me this evening were a bit on the elderly side and asked if I could show them some of the workings of the new car they were about to embark in? And even though it was indeed a ploy to get me to haul their luggage to the car, they heard my heartfelt, "Yes, ma'am, I'll be happy to show you to your car, and may as well take some of those suitcases also."

With this decision I was not able to exit immediately to my left as would've happened otherwise, with my new friend still impatiently waiting on his ride to wherever in my roommate's car with me as his chauffeur. "Hey. Buddy. Gotta show these ladies to their new car; be back in a minute. We're still good."

As the two lady renters and I weaved our way through the crowd, all of a sudden I heard a voice say, "Well, hey there, Ole Skippy, fancy running into you here. Hey, everybody, look who it is. None other than federal fugitive Skippy Sanders in the flesh and on the run for the past two years."

It was my probation officer from back in South Carolina. Flying into Reno on a government funded vacation or seminar on how to continue to bilk the public out of their cash. My federal probation officer from the Jackpot trials the decade prior who was in charge of my twenty-five-year special probation period as part of my initial ten-year federal sentence. Even though at this time I had been indicted by the State of South Carolina and tried by the State of South Carolina, I was officially still on federal probation because my status was never one of being incarcerated in the state system up to this juncture, which just at that second drastically changed. My probation officer, whose real name is Mark, was just sorta standing there waiting for a shuttle to Lake Tahoe with a group of about a dozen or so others flying in from South and North Carolina. He announced to the rest of the agents there that he intended to have a word with me and then placed me in custody. I explained to him what was going down—that I was taking these two little old ladies and their luggage out to their freshly rented Intrepid. Mark announced to his compatriots that we were going to take a step outside and that we would be back shortly, and with that, he looked at me and said, "Well, let's go." Even helped me carry some of their luggage, and off we went with the two little ladies tagging behind us.

The two little old ladies asked me what was going on, and I told them I just signed up for a little federal assistance program. And wouldn't you know it, just about now the guy needing the ride in my roommate's junked-up car approaches our little group and asks me if everything's all right, to which I respond, "No, everything ain't alright worth a shit. Our deal is off." OK, keep in mind we're standing there with a federal agent. A federal agent becoming more and more concerned by the second.

He said, "OK, Skippy, whose this crab?" I told him it was some guy I was giving a ride to after my shift. Mark looked at this guy and said something to the effect of, "You have exactly five seconds to demonstrate that you are of the mindset to retreating or face a wrath of authority like you have never witnessed. Am I clear?"

This guy, this idiot, steps toward this federal agent with just a very slight half-step lunge, trying to explain to the agent that his only way to get to where he needed to go was me as no one would rent him a car. At this point I was on Mark's side, just wishing this dweeb would simply vanish. The agent said in a firm voice something to the effect of "This is your final warning." He whipped out his badge and said further, "I am a United States federal agent. And I hereby order you to fall back. Now."

Let me tell you people one thing. When it comes to authority, when it comes to your assessing odds against coming out on top when challenging the type of authority that I have witnessed, namely federal marshals, probation officers, and most officers under the color of law in general, you do not want to go there. Now, you might be able to pull off outwitting them or even outrunning them, but trust me when I tell you, your stupid ass is in no way going to out muscle them. You don't know the meaning of a formally trained federal officer. They are from another planet, trained first and foremost for their own survival. Trained in order to facilitate that survival to act in unison with one another, and just do not have it in their demeanor to accept any type of bullshit challenge from any type of subject of their attention in any type of manner. Period. Law enforcement in general is categorically unmatched when it gets right down to the jungle ethics of strength and just who the fcuk is in charge. It ain't us. Any of us. No matter how badass somebody portrays himself to be, when it comes down to the nitty and the gritty, we ain't got no shot. I had sense enough to realize this and never once challenged them face-to-face. It's why I'm still alive. Throughout the course of their pursuit of me, their apprehension, and transport of my stupid ass back to South Carolina, no games were to be played. The occasional uprisings we hear of in prisons or on the streets due to perceived violations of one's civil or social rights are all what you call temporary and meaningless.

Anyway, after agent Mark ran off my would-be hatchet murderer in the desert somewhere on a horse with loose change, we proceeded out to the car rental area with the two old ladies and their baggage. How did all this happen? A dream, maybe? Oh yeah, being escorted by a federal agent who's allowing me to follow through on renting this car to somebody and helping these two elderly ladies to be on their way. During the course of the next few minutes, I proceeded to pack these ladies' luggage in the trunk, showed them how to open and close the trunk, and even went so far as to start the car and show them certain nuances of the brand-new Dodge Intrepid. For a very brief snapshot, I found myself in the driver's seat with Special Agent Mark standing by the right front fender. It hit me then that, despite our predicament, Special Agent Mark trusted me. To an extent. And for that, any ridiculous notion of making a clean break for it was instantly taken off the table. Which goes to show that whenever someone implies a certain trust in you, it should be your business not to disavow that trust. Or maybe I was just a little bit too pussy to hit that gas petal and get the hell out of there. Whatever the reason, I didn't do it. Whatever the reason, I did not flip on anybody doing my criminal prosecution. The same me. The same DNA. The same gratitude is indeed my DNA, regardless of what you might think or what actually motivates it.

Chapter 34
Can I Whine Just a Little?

Stupid asses. To exist in amazement of another's circumstances, abilities, and achievements is quite simple and mildly entertaining in and of itself, but it contains nothing of substance for ya, my friend. We do it all the time. I discovered many people intrigued by those of us involved in the trade, to the point where they might like to be a druggie smuggling slug on the one hand, but then in an instant are relieved that they're not. Relief that we're all just normal ole Square D Joes. This especially applies to some of us involved a bit higher up in the weed culture. Like me. Not planned. Not expected. Simply overly intrigued about access to what seemed practically unlimited money, gals, toys, or freedom (all vastly exaggerated to begin with). Nothing of substance. Then, thankfully, the fantasy comes to an abrupt end, and then comes the spending—or wasting—of a chunk of my life doing my time amid the world's ultimate throwaways in shiny new prisons.

The drug smuggling culture mimics many such other hustles, for it basks in the intrigue of risk and all the associated rewards. You know...it's the illusion of it all. It's however one chooses to spin it, whatever serves and fits. Risk is a great excuse when it needs to be so that we might elect to remain disassociated. To either side? Instant money—found money—contains the basis for nearly all the intrigue and is, to a significant degree, quite similar to the fantasy aspects we subscribe to when pondering the chances of winning a lottery; how much easier it is to entertain mere thoughts than to actually offer up anything entertaining. Think about music and sports for a sec. While they're not illegal, it's a crying shame how many of us devote ungodly chunks of time to such arenas that offer nothing for us but the entertainment itself. It's due to the big money. Big dust. Smuggling drugs is very similar, except for the fact that it's something most anybody can do; no special talent or skill required. When the intrigue becomes glamorous, it becomes pragmatic to render drugs so exorbitant in penalties that the government can come after smugglers, can seize their easy money, and present the "local hoodlum element" types as ones to be put away. It's called a reverse opportunity. And I found that the basis for this opportunity has much to do with this book's opening line.

My stupid ass went to trial three times. Two fed, one state. One fed acquittal, which should have negated the second fed trial under the double jeopardy clause, but whatever another fed trial with conviction, then in round number two, a separate state grand jury pursuit, indictment, and conviction a decade later. In each case it was the government's strategy to prop up the popular misconceptions of the biz as all dependent on the notion, "Well, you broke the law." The primary objective of the state was and has remained constant to this day: for any and every defendant to enter a plea of guilty, particularly in all victimless crimes (which should not allow for prosecution to begin with).

Chapter 35
All Good Things Must Pass: Bye-Bye

Ever notice how sweet the first line of some songs are? Those first lines tend to set the entire song up and sometimes leave the listener longing to crank. Don't go cranking, OK? Read something, OK? Here's the best thing I found out about books, and this comes from a guy who has never read very much. With a song, you might not always have complete control over where you hear it or what's going on when you do. A book is different. You have more control over where and under what circumstances you read it. Even if it's in prison, one gets to choose where a book may be enjoyed or absorbed. And that first line in a book sets up the mood for anticipation. I read a few books in my time…and during some of my time too. The bed was usually a safe place for me to read in the big house as I would suppose it is for many. Hey, for some of us on the outside, it represents most of the enjoyment we're able to garner from bed anymore. But anyway, my most vivid memory of reading a good book occurred quite unexpectedly, and it is to this particular episode that the book you are reading right now is attributable.

The longer one spends in the big house, the more one learns how to manipulate the system. There's a common religion in there. We would mostly worship it in silence. Hope became our salvation. Became our Yellow Brick Road to salvation. A significant part of enduring hope is a degree of security and maybe a little bit of happiness. Back to this roommate thing. I had several roommates over the years who greatly contributed to these concerns. Sure, I look back at all of us as similarly situated men trying to make the best of it and trying to get our happy asses back through the front gate. Not over it, not under it, not around it. Through it.

It was another Sunday night, one of the 624 Sunday nights my ass was stuck in there. I had had another quite busy day of running numbers and taking bets on, mainly, the NFL games that day and a good many more on NASCAR. You'd be surprised at how much action there was to be had in NASCAR. I certainly was. As the evening was winding down and that last Sunday night game was about to end, the handful of winners would come down to my room to claim their winning tickets. They knocked; I let 'em in, paid them their winnings, and asked them to ride out for I didn't have time to discuss anything because there were others lining up to be paid also. It was during these particular episodes that my roommates would have to endure these constant interruptions. We worked out deals with each other, usually where the "house" would provide all the groceries since that was what everybody used as currency to bet if they agreed to prepare the in-room meals and keep the place clean. It worked out for years like this because who in their right mind wouldn't want to eat free? So most roommates accepted a few interruptions of their peaceful Saturday and Sunday evenings in exchange for a full belly of basically free food, which we would consume after that last count of the evening.

This is when everyone is locked down in their ten-by-ten rooms as there is usually no movement on the rock except for a couple of runarounds cleaning the place up and a guard or two on patrol.

However, my roommate at this time was one discussed earlier; he lived under a bridge previously and was locked up in here for arson. A very unique individual with plenty of good sense, seemingly what we'd refer to as a normal type of guy. Well, one of the last inmates—gentlemen, if you will—to come to the door that evening just before lockdown at ten o'clock wanted to borrow some food so he and his roommate could prepare a setup after lockdown just as we were doing. Now this guy was more your typical penitentiary nuisance-ass nobody. Having burned every bridge he ever crossed, including mine, with no support from the outside, including family, and no respect from the inside. Too fucking stupid to ever have a job, much less a business or a hustle, and perfectly content to assert his ilk upon all those around him. A true piece of shit. A mental case. Prison is home for many mentally sick people. Society simply does not have any interest to treat them, so they just lock their asses up. This very deterrence the establishment, administrative, and bureaucratic types depend upon to influence the rest of us that we need to avoid prison at all costs. This guy lent much credence to the culturally accepted strategy so employed. 'Course, I opened the door and asked, "What do you want this time, yo?"

To which he said that he had a winning ticket but lost it and said it came from his roommate and they would like to be paid. He said that before he knew I would not accept the ticket from him, that I wanted nothing to do with his sorry mental ass. But there he was, at five minutes till standing roll call count was to ensue, and there I was having won about two hundred bucks' worth of food that weekend, saying something to the effect of, the extent of his bleeding humanity notwithstanding, "Come on, man, don't you still owe me a chunk from a couple weeks ago? We both know you didn't win shit. Why can't you go out and find your own hustle? Listen, just gimme a break, OK? So no. Not giving you anything; just ride the fcuk out. Enough already."

At which point I hear the same thing again: "You know, Skippy, one day a MF going to stop you." Listen. I have no doubt that's a true statement. But guess what. Today ain't the day, and you damn sure ain't the MF. So beat it; beat it.

Well, the guy just sort of stood there very sad looking to the point where I might've notice him slightly well up. Or was it me? Here stood a human being. With no hope. No shot. No life. Hell, there had been times I had been flat broke on the Sunday evening rock and had gone around and tried to drum up some food. But I would pay them back. Wouldn't pester the guys. Wouldn't plot to break into their rooms.

All of a sudden, my roommate, Gatyam, said, "Hey, Skippy, were you planning to offer me any food tonight?"

"Well, not really because you never accept it."

And on this night, my roommate asked out of the bleu if he could provide this inmate at the door enough food as to go do his own setup. Well sure, and we slipped this dude a few items, and off he went just in time for the ten o'clock standing count.

Thirty minutes later, after count, Gatyam was helping me clean up from the meal he had eaten none of, and we were watching a little TV, and I had to ask, "After all the nights we spent together in this cell, not once have you accepted the first bite, the first crumb of food from me. This four-hundred-day run just ended as you asked me to give food to somebody else. Somebody you know firsthand to be a nuisance piece of shit and who will only come back wanting more and more." Ole Gatyam didn't say much else; just sort of climbed up into the top bunk as we watched television and worked on crossword puzzles. It was then that I attempted to enlist conversation with this very strange roommate of mine, perhaps even trying to rile him up a little bit just to get some kind of response or explanation.

I said, "You know most people in this world more so resemble him than they do you. Are you with me? Sorry. Useless. And above all else, just plain stupid. Every time I meet someone new, my hope is, well, maybe this is the one exception. This guy. But guess what? It doesn't happen. Why extend a clean slate to a new face when damn near one hundred percent of the time they're going to disappoint? Why do we fight it? Let me tell you, Gatyam, I truly believe the world is running out of good people. Wish I knew there was hope for just one good person who might come along and offer up some good for goodness' sake."

And with that, my roommate leaned over his top bunk, looking straight down at me, and said, "Well, Skippy, here's why I gave that man some food. Some of your food. And here is an answer for you regarding whether or not this world has any good people left in it, giving us all hope such types still exist.

"One very cold night years ago, before being able to claim a permanent spot under a bridge in North Charleston, I was forced one night to find shelter in a parking garage in downtown Charleston. And out of the blue a very beautiful young woman, like an angel, appeared and told me not to give up, and that my bad times would soon end. It was if this comforting soul had sought me out. If I ever lost my faith, it was granted back to me that night. This woman was being hurried along by her date and told me she would be right back. Thirty minutes later she returned with a plate of hot food offered up by one of the top restaurants in Charleston. It was obviously intended for her, but there she was presenting it to me. I told her I couldn't accept it and to get back to her party. At this point she slipped me two twenty dollar bills and the keys to some bed-and-breakfast that I never went to or stayed in. As she departed, she wiped a tear with her forefinger, kissed it, and touched me with an elegant finger on this very same cheek right here. I mattered that night, Skippy. Somebody gave a shit for no reason at all, and I have never been the same since. Good night."

OMG. Well, neither have I. Nobody was looking in my little window that evening. So, what do ya know. Turns out there is no use in painting the window after all.

About the Author

Skippy Rast is a former drug smuggler whose memoir uDam Skippy exposes the secret lessons and some darkness of an often glamorized lifestyle. Through an irreverent, uncouth style, he aims to reveal the true colors of the streets while attempting to provide readers with something other than mere entertainment.